The Fred Dagg Scripts

The Fred Dagg Scripts

With cartoons by Patrick Cook

Nelson

Thomas Nelson Australia
480 La Trobe Street Melbourne Victoria 3000

First published 1981
Reprinted 1981 (twice), 1982 (three times)
Copyright © Roderick Willows Pty Ltd, 1981
Copyright illustrations © Patrick Cook, 1981

National Library of Australia
Cataloguing-in-Publication Data

The Fred Dagg scripts.

  Radio scripts by John Clarke, illustrated by
  Patrick Cook.
  ISBN 0 17 006072 1.

  I. Fred Dagg (Radio program). I. Clarke, John.
  II. Cook, Patrick, 1949—

791.44'72

Typeset by ProComp Productions Pty Ltd, Adelaide.
Printed by Globe Press, Fitzroy, Victoria.

CONTENTS

INTRODUCTION

Publications of this type have Introductions. Not because the reading public asks for them, or needs them, or benefits from them, but because publishers feel that the reading public requires them, expects them, and learns from them. They provide a context.

I think we can all see how silly this is. If it is not clear from the cover what the book is, the proper response is not to explain things in an Introduction, it is to redesign the cover. If the fact that the author has written the book is not thought to be a sufficient definition of the author, then it is time someone got in touch with base.

For the record, Mr Dagg has published no collections of poetry, has never been a visiting fellow in any formal sense, and has no interests.

THE ECONOMIC OUTLOOK: FEBRUARY 1980

The day-to-day business of government has become very difficult in the 1980s, so it has been replaced by a long-running discussion about economics . . .

Gidday. Now I regret to have to inform you that the buffeting the stock market's been taking in the last week or so is by no means entirely played out.

Of course the bull-trend in recent times has tended to over-value certain indices and a bit of a topple in the mining and oil and gas sectors has been imminent for some time.

In fact it'll come as no surprise to close observers that I personally vacated the vast bulk of my portfolio in the pre-Xmas rush, and plunged heavily into Governmental Hysteria which boomed more or less overnight due to exploratory drilling in Election Futures. I've never been of the 'I told you so' persuasion but some sort of explanation is required, and I did see it coming, so if you're at all interested in the interpretation of someone who's just cleaned up, here's an artist's impression of what went on.

There's an increasing acceptance of the view that by permitting overseas money to enter the market by the megaoodle, we are buying into gold-related inflation based in certain areas where the population falls to its knees every couple of hours and worships ice-hockey.

Whether or not this is true, it is certainly true that American inflation slipped out of the laboratory last Thursday and hasn't been seen since. The idea of actually controlling inflation, which is like trying to stop a runaway train by offering the driver a housing loan, has now been abandoned altogether, and American banks are getting their interest rates out of the phone book.

What this means for Australia is that unfortunately after the economy's been dressed up for its electoral outing, it might have to be stripped back to the chassis and completely re-designed.

I'm very much afraid that the idea of an inverse relationship between inflation and unemployment has gone out the window, and although I think we can still blame this on the unemployed and Henry II, we can't keep talking rubbish forever, and sooner or later we're going to have to work out what's going on.

OIL PRICING POLICY

Oil Pricing Policy has been one of the
highlights of the modern age. It shows
every sign of becoming a classic.

Gidday. Now there's a great deal of talk about at the moment on the general subject of oil parity, and basically there are two sides to the argument, with the statuesque Malcolm standing in the affirmative and Bill Hayden captaining the 'no thank you's'.

The question centres around the fact that Australia pulls a good deal of the slimy additive out of a hole in the Basso Profundo, and the main problem is whether this should be charged out to the consumer at the same rate as the stuff we buy in by the truckload from areas up near where the Shah used to play a lot of his tennis.

There are those who say that if we're growing it out behind the bike-shed, the only possible advantage is in our facility to lower the price and stop pretending it's all flown in from Paris every morning in festive wrapping.

And the contrary view is that because there's only about a pint-and-a-half of it under the blue surges, we can't encourage unfettered use of it, and that by using the price to the consumer as a governor, we can prevent that and return to the state a certain amount of money which will enable direct taxation to be lowered or stabilised. Or if they choose not to do that, they will at least be able to buy more F111's and thereby continue their close exploration of the seabed.

The other element in all of this is foreign exchange, because of course by syphoning oil out of the sea, we militate against the consistent drain on funds paid to people who live on the other side of the recently imperilled Indian Ocean.

You can make your own mind up about all of this, but I should point out you haven't got long. The world's oil supply is destined to run out next Wednesday. However, if the oil companies find they've still got a couple of billion barrels at a slightly higher price, I must ask you not to be surprised.

OVERSEAS INVESTMENT

Overseas investment in Australia has reached new levels in the 1980s, and people are clearly wondering why. Not all people, only a few. Australians mostly.

Gidday. Now I suppose you've all seen, as I have, reports in the tissues about the boom we're experiencing in overseas investment.

This is a very complicated area, and I think it's as well to have a bit of a look at the causes and methods involved before you find your back garden is fetching a new high on the Hong Kong exchange. And, as the international finance manager of Open Slather Ltd, I'm probably in as good a position as anyone to explain the whole thing to you.

Open Slather is a reasonable enough example of what's going on. We were involved initially in the rubber business in the part underneath the thin bit in South America, and then we diversified into the sugar field in Africa, and we invested the profits in various enterprising projects in Europe and Asia. Then England went into what I can only describe as a fairly steep decline and we shifted a good deal of capital into South Africa, where as you know the economic equation is particularly well-served by some pretty inexpensive labour.

The problem there is that it's now widely recognised that one of these days there's going to be a strike in South Africa, and when I say strike, I mean to invoke more the notion of total war than the rather less catastrophic idea of picketing.

Given the uncertainty that marks the future in South Africa, we began looking about for another pillow to put the tooth under.

What we were looking for was a place which was crawling with natural resources which we could process, because of course the people who process natural resources tend to make slightly more money out of it than the people who stand out in the sun all day harvesting stuff and putting it under the trees in boxes.

We wanted a country with stable government, and we have every expectation of Malcolm's continued stewardship.

We wanted it away from the world's trouble-spots, somewhere where the public doesn't care too much about what's going on and where the legislation is written only with a very light pencil.

And Australia's perfect. Most of the people live in the bottom right-hand corner and we're left with a place the size of Western Europe in which to charge about with a front-end loader and a big sack.

THATCHER'S MONETARISM

It became obvious at an early stage that the Thatcher Government was unwell. Explanations were called for, reasons sought, opinions canvassed.

Gidday. Now I can see just from a quick glance around the room that you're all just as surprised as I am to see that Margaret Thatcher seems to be taking a fair bit of water and is having a certain amount of trouble with the crew.

The main reason for this change of fortune appears to be economic, and in order to understand roughly what's going on, it's important to realise that the Thatcher philosophy is monetarist. Nobody knows what this means but it's important to realise it if you want to go on and try for the car.

The implication is of course that there's some opposition in Margaret's mind to the notion of overweaning fiscal policy. But no one knows what that means either, except that she's probably fundamentally anti-Keynesian, which again isn't as helpful as it might be, because poor old Maynard's been fairly quiet since the war, and it's even been suggested that he exhibited a bit of a liquidity preference and the family had to keep him tucked away in a little parabola somewhere in Hampshire.

Friedman's probably the key to the whole business, except that he's extremely unlikely to admit it.

But for what it's worth, monetary policy works like this. I forget the aim of it, but this is how it does it. The amount of money in circulation can be controlled to some extent by various governmental actions. They can alter the lending rate of the central bank, or control bank lending generally. They can grab big sacks of money from banks and other lending institutions and remove it from circulation. They can sneak up behind people who hoard money at home and put it back into circulation by leaving it on trains. Or they can take it out of circulation altogether by simply not printing any more and just waiting till the old stuff is too floppy to use properly.

But the most important instrument of monetary policy is the facility to remove huge amounts by paying them into a special account labelled 'Milton Friedman, to collect'.

Whatever it is, it doesn't work. And if Margaret isn't very careful, no one else will either.

AN ANOMALY IN THE PUBLIC ACCOUNT

The technological highlight of 1980 came in April, when it was discovered that the Federal Government had given away $285 million to the nation's chemists. For six years, every chemist in Australia had been receiving $6000 per annum. The mistake was attributed to a computer, rather than to a chemist, or to a government.

Gidday. Now I don't want to make excuses.

The $285 million we gave away to the chemistry set was certainly a mistake, and I'm very much afraid that under the finder's keeper's legislation we can't actually get any of it back. And the idea that they'll come forward voluntarily and give it back is out of the question; because of course they've probably become accustomed to its face by now and have come to regard an extra $6000 a year floating in out of nowhere as a standard item of capital inflow, and they're all working very hard and nobody's indispensary and whichever way you look at it the money has gone and it does look like the work of professionals.

I don't want to try to pull the boycott over anyone's eyes here. Mistakes have been made, and I'll be the first to admit that, for a government which is trying to cut down public spending, to leave $285 million in its other trousers is certainly something of an embarrassment, although we did appoint people to look for anomalies like this and it's a relief to me personally that they came up with this discovery before the public sector was gazetted and we had to start borrowing from chemists to keep essential services running.

However, on the other hand, the news is not all gloom and despond. Very real advances have been made in other areas. A quite colossal saving has been made in the area of Employment and Youth Affairs. Ian's lads look like coming in well under budget and at the moment it looks as if we're talking here of underspending by about $25 million, and we cut the NEAT allocation by nearly 50 per cent last year, so there's an outside possibility that the department might actually declare a profit for the seasonally adjusted June quarter.

If we'd cut the allowance to chemists and then underpaid them by a further $25 million and had some maverick computer spitting out $285 million on employment schemes, we might have picked the mistake up sooner.

We might not have, of course, but it's interesting to speculate. Any chemist will tell you that.

NELSON BUNKER HUNT

People often think life is easy for the very wealthy. This is a lot of pish tosh, and from time to time a cruel and tragic example is presented.

Gidday. Now I'd like to have a few words with you about the rather curious circumstances in which my very dear close personal friend Nelson Bunker Hunt seems to have taken up residence.

I don't talk about this solely out of a concern for the unfortunate few who lack the initiative to make a success of themselves in a free market economy, and more particularly of course by cornering the free market economy. I mention it really only because he's a neighbour of ours.

11

He's got about 10000 square kilometres of Australia, which in acres is equivalent to something in the region of about Cyprus. He grabbed a few cattle stations in Queensland last year and for some time now he's owned either the Northern Part or the Territory section of the Northern Territory, and I must say it disheartens me considerably to read that he and his brother might have dropped about 7 or 8 billion before lunch on Thursday. Particularly in view of what they had to do to earn it in the first place.

If you think it's easy spending thirty years not getting offside with your father, then you'll probably never know true wealth. And the Hunt boys might not either if the commodity prices are anything to go by.

Apparently what the lads used to do was buy silver futures, and instead of selling them again or training them to do a few elementary tricks around the home, they'd hang on to them and wait for the silver to arrive.

And what this meant was that as they had more and more silver sitting around the office, the price of the silver they didn't have went up, because the bulk of the world's supply was hidden in the bunker.

When the price of the silver they didn't own went up, the price of the stuff they did own tended to go up with it.

Then the other day someone took the unprecedented step of asking them to pay for something. So they're going to have to come up with some actual money, which is a middle-class substitute for wealth.

Still, it might mean we have a new neighbour up north, perhaps a nice Japanese family conglomerate or a German or something.

Or maybe they'll take a stand this time and refuse to allow ownership to go out of the country, and just sell it to another American.

MINING AND SACRED SITES

It is clearly urgent that the question of mining and sacred sites be addressed. Australia is unequivocal on the matter of human rights in Africa, in Russia and Eastern Europe, in South America, in parts of Asia and on Saturn. There remains, however, widespread misunderstanding about any human rights that might be thought to exist in Australia.

Gidday. Now there's been a great deal of talk recently about the troubled business of sacred sites and how to pull the ground out from under them. And I think it's become quite clear by now that until we have some proper discussion about the cultural and historical aspects of the problem, it's going to be very difficult for us to formulate a consistent philosophy.

The main stumbling block at the moment seems to be a determined refusal to understand exactly what these sacred sites actually mean to the people concerned. And why the Aboriginal people are unable to grasp this I don't know.

The white man's deeply religious concern for certain sections of the sweeping plain is fairly well documented by now, as are the complex and arcane rituals associated with the worship of the land and its mystical properties.

In fact the company I'm connected with in Western Australia, Mystical Properties Ltd, has published a very tasteful coffee-table book, explaining everything from the exploratory drilling phase, or the Dreamtime as we call it, right through to the final extraction of the worshipful essence itself and the imprecations that go on in the temples until the primitive chanting of the closing prices.

These books have been given away to the Aboriginal people in the region as part of a programme of education which culminates in the taking of communion.

In fact only recently, as you might have seen in the press if they bothered to print anything favourable to us, we flew into the area with 44-gallon drums of wine and gave it away to the Aboriginal people in a gesture as old as time itself.

So I don't think anyone can say we haven't bent over backwards to explain what is admittedly perhaps a slightly metaphysical attitude to the land. I really think we've done all we can.

If these people persistently refuse to comprehend the strange and secret workings of Mystical Properties Ltd, I'm afraid our culture might disappear altogether.

Either that, or theirs will, and theirs is older, so I wouldn't be surprised if it's we who have to go underground for a while.

FOREIGN OWNERSHIP

The government's policy on overseas ownership is theoretically sound. Only when put into practice does it appear to be in any sort of trouble.

Gidday. Now I know a lot of people haven't always agreed with me, and I must say I've come to regard this as a very healthy sign. And nowhere, I think, has it been healthier than in the general area of foreign ownership.

Certainly we haven't been without our problems in this area, and despite what I've read in some of the more salacious wrappers, the trouble has not revolved to any extent around the power of multi-national corporations, whose role in the affairs of this country is in fact virtually nil.

The main problem has been in reaching general agreement amongst ourselves about precisely what is meant by the term 50 per cent. It's a dangerously vague term and it should probably have been whipped out while the act was still being drafted. But we've tried to give the term some meaning from time to time by dressing it up as something else and taking it for a walk around the exchange.

Of course every now and again we lower the boom pretty severely.

15

We did this recently in Adelaide and the overseas interests are still smarting from the suddenness and the severity of the rebuff.

I think it's only fair that you know exactly what happened, and perhaps more importantly why it happened, because there's a principle at stake here and I often think that if people looked for the principles inherent in action taken by government, then at least they'd be fully occupied, and we could get on with it.

The pharmaceutical industry in Australia was under direct threat, and although no-one's quite sure what 50 per cent is, somebody in the Treasury told us he was pretty sure it was in excess of 6 per cent. And this 6 per cent was what overseas interests were looking to buy.

Now 6 per cent of an entire industry is probably going to run into money sooner or later, and for this reason we looked very carefully at the whole suggestion.

We then discovered that they already owned 94 per cent and that 6 per cent would give them total control, an idea which had a certain symmetrical ring to it and would put the foreign holding at the 50 per cent requirement, twice.

Ultimately we had to knock the takeover on the head because giving the chemistry set $235 million to spend on an industry that was 100 per cent overseas owned was thought to be a major risk to our reserves and to peg the ownership at 94 per cent seemed like a responsible thing to do.

If we keep 6 per cent, we'll at least get a newsletter at the end of June.

EXCESSIVE PROFITS IN THE OIL INDUSTRY

In this troubled age, even the corporate
sector feels responsible to the people.
Dialogue has been established, and a frank
exchange of ideas has ensued.

Gidday. Now I'd like to have a word or two with you about the performance of Lubradagg over the past year. As you know, the oil industry has come in for some pretty severe criticism recently for making amounts of money that are said to be excessive, although I've been making them for long enough now to be able to say quite openly that there's nothing excessive about them.

But I can't expect poor people to understand this. It's getting to the point where we're feeling a little bit embarrassed about announcing how well we're doing.

I explained last time that our profit levels are dictated to us by OPEC, and I think most people have accepted this. But I see one of our competitors has come up with a new idea. They announced their profit, which was about $40 million, and then they said that this was illusory, which I initially assumed meant that they couldn't lose it. But on further reading I gather that they were actually claiming that in some sense the $40 million was an illusion.

This was picked up by a couple of our other competitors and this put the amount of money that didn't really exist up to about $170 million.

The reason that it's illusory is rather complicated. Most of the profit is in the form of paper money, as distinct from share certificates, mortgages, cheques and bank-notes which tend to be made more of paper. And also of course, profits are illusory in the oil business because of the breathtaking cost of exploration. In other words, you don't have a wage if there's something you'd like to buy with it.

I hope you've got all this, because if we can get off the front page within a couple of years, we'd like to announce what we've really made, which is even less excessive.

THE NUGAN HAND BANK INQUIRY

In their attempts to serve the public, governments have occasionally left the body of the meeting and become involved in other things. When this has happened, explanations have cleared the air immediately.

THE VIETNAM VETERAN NATIONAL PARTY STOCKBROKING BALLISTICS EXPERT WHO THOUGHT NUGAN HAND WAS A GREYHOUND

Gidday. Now I'd like to have a word or two with you about the rather unfortunate publicity we've been getting lately over certain activities with which we apparently have some sort of very faint connection.

Probably the most notable of these has been the substantial investment some of our branches seem to have made with the Sleight of Hand Bank.

In fact if I can take that point up straight away, the Bank itself has been allowed to trade its way into difficulties, but apparently even the answer-phone was lying about its age and by the time the authorities got down there, all that was left was a book of instructions. You put your money in through a little door at the top, selected the temperature and length of the wash you were after, and put your powder in at various stages during the cycle.

For very delicate amounts and stuff that was really filthy, it was advisable to go for the hand-wash first. We're not quite sure how this worked at the moment, but you could put a dollar in here and pick it up either at the Hong Kong or the Leger de Main branch in Paris, and it wouldn't even remember its name.

But this really hasn't got anything much to do with us. We were simply looking for a safe investment to protect the little man, and it's unfortunate that no one can actually find the little man, but that isn't our fault either.

We don't know what happened. I don't really see how we can be expected to know too much about what's going on. We're the government. If you want to know what's going on in Australian business, you ask an Australian businessman. You go to Brazil, and you ask one.

MORE ON NUGAN HAND

> It is suggested, from time to time, that people have behaved badly in order to acquire more adequate funding. These suggestions are invariably wrong, and can be put right quite easily.

Gidday. Now about these amounts of money I'm supposed to have received from various agencies of the Sleight of Hand Bank and, before we go any further, let me repudiate utterly any connection at all with the credit wing of the organisation: Blankcard.

This was not my idea and in fact it wasn't a facility I ever had a great deal of occasion to use.

The travel refund I was paid in April of last year, I did receive, although it wasn't $375000, it was $37.50, and on top of that it was late. The house I was given in the Bahamas wasn't a house, and it wasn't given to me. It was a houseboat, or more correctly it was an ocean-going yacht, and it didn't have a false keel, and if it did there wasn't anything in it. And if there was, it wasn't any sort of drug, and if it was, it certainly wasn't put there by me. And I didn't take it out either. I've never seen the boat. I don't even really own it. It's owned by the Maritime Hire Company. Of which I'm not a director. Very much. Any more. I was, but only very briefly and not since the war, and I have no knowledge of anyone connected with it now, and the fact that I haven't seen them for years has got nothing to do with the fact that no one else has either. I didn't see them for years before that.

The idea that I can be dragged into disrepute by a lot of unsubstantiated rumours runs against everything I've come to respect about this country. I don't see why we don't all just sit back and wait for the findings of the next inquiry. These things are properly constituted and availed of the full power of the law. Perhaps the stated brief of the last commission was a little narrow. Perhaps a full commission set up to establish the date and a long range weather forecast is only a beginning. But I think it's a good beginning. And I have every confidence that the next inquiry will go a good deal further. Although perhaps not as far as I'll be going.

NOONKANBAH

The Noonkanbah dispute forced the question of Aboriginal land rights into the public arena. While it was being discussed, the mining company, Amax, borrowed drilling equipment from CSR, and went about its business. The governments of Western Australia and the nation were each less responsible than the other. A simple misunderstanding.

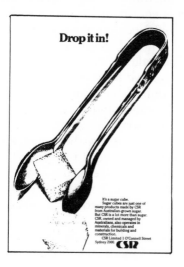

Drop it in!

It's a sugar cube.
Sugar cubes are just one of many products made by CSR from Australian-grown sugar. But CSR is a lot more than sugar. CSR, owned and managed by Australians, also operates in minerals, chemicals and materials for building and construction.
CSR Limited 1 O'Connell Street Sydney 2000. **CSR**

Gidday. Now for some of you slower characters out there who have still got question marks in your speech bubbles over this Noonkanbah business, a couple of facts have come to light, and I think a proper understanding might result from some consideration of them.

Of one of them anyway. I think the fact that CSR have launched an advertising campaign headed by the remarkably catchy and highly topical expression 'Drop it in', is probably entirely coincidental. I don't imagine the term 'Drop it in' refers to anything other than sugar cubes. In fact there are a couple of sugar cubes pictured in the adverts with a member of the Tong dynasty, just in case anyone thinks 'Drop it in' might be a reference to anything else they do.

I see from the ad for instance that they're involved in mineral operations, but you don't drop minerals in, you pull them out and give them to Amax or whoever else is mentioned in the Court Circular. So there'd be no real need to advertise at all.

But the major insight was provided by the Australian Ambassador when he was putting his case to a UN sub-committee on something called discrimination. He made a couple of points of enormous importance.

The first was that Noonkanbah was an exception. Which is true, and anyone who doesn't accept it doesn't know what's good for me. The rule is, of course, that Aboriginals and mining companies have been able to negotiate agreements, and I don't know quite what constitutes a rule but if a string of exceptions and a subcommittee in Geneva don't go awfully close I think it's time someone got in touch with Hoyle.

Federal intervention was also discussed, and it was pointed out that the power to intervene is a discretionary one and it would be a question of judgement as to whether or not the government ought to use it. I don't know what discretion and judgement are paying on the Stock Exchange but I've certainly never heard of them.

I hope I've made myself clear on this question. Aside from anything else we need more oil so we can tax you on it.

THE BUDGET

The Federal budget is a complex document, and the public often fails to grasp some of its more subtle aspects.

Gidday. Now I'd like to have a word or two with you today about the rather bizarre press coverage of our recent budget. I don't know what we've got to do to make people understand what we're trying to do up here.

Perhaps if we wrote the estimates out with a big crayon and dangled them over the country from balloons and light aircraft, someone might grasp the very odd inkling of what's going on.

I think it's time you woke up to yourselves. There's no point in having the young fellow standing around sticking his finger in and out of the hole in the dyke if all you people are going to do is wander about the place being grumpy.

Running the country is just like running a household, and I don't know whether you've ever had your household run by the Labor Party, but after about eighteen months the whole place lifts completely off the ground and unless you got down on a travel grant before they introduced hydraulic round-the-clock inflation, you'll find yourself spending less and less time with your family.

And as you know, this is precisely the position we inherited. We've been able to patch up bits of it since we got in certainly, but Rome wasn't built in the whole of the post-war period with a three year gap, and there are elements of the way things are going at the moment that would disturb anyone. But I do wish people wouldn't get so disturbed about them.

Work is the thing that'll pull this country out of the already superb position it's in now to an even better position. People have simply got to realise that only by working extremely hard and not stopping all the time to ask for more money or part of a condition, can we improve the state of this country. Well, some of the states of this country. Some of the other states I'm afraid we'll have to mark as absent.

But we can't be expected to look after everything anyway. You can't look after everyone. You've got to have priorities. We've got a list somewhere of the people we've been looking after. I haven't actually got it myself at the moment. Tony Staley's got it. He's taking treatment for it but as far as I know, he's still got it, and if your name doesn't appear on it, I must ask you to stop looking out the window and just get on with your work, or whatever it is you people do with your time.

AN EXPORT UPTURN

Figures often lie, of course, and the truth is
clear only when a full explanation
is presented.

Gidday. Now I don't know whether or not you noticed this, but Australia's exports earned 33 per cent more this year than they did last year, and before the waiting room fills up again I might as well answer the obvious question for you.

If exports are up to record levels and the economy's in such encouraging fettle, why haven't we all got jobs and why aren't we all making a fortune and having the time of our lives?

We are. I haven't had such a good time in years and the money I've made this year has become something of a joke around the estate. I don't know where we're going to hide it all. The outbuildings are already groaning with incentive payments and the builders are due in any day now to throw together some sort of shelter for the actual export returns.

Of course it'll be some time before the recovery is complete and we can take the straps off your bits of the economy as well. In the meantime I must ask you to be patient, and for those of you who already are patients, I'm afraid the cost of your medical insurance has been forced up by the unions and the Russian threat, and the team of close-pattern-formation violinists will be around to pick up the increment this afternoon.

Perhaps I should have mentioned earlier that the recovery I've been talking about in the Australian economy is capital intensive rather than labour intensive, and what this means is that people who've invested well during the last few years are now receiving an income which is indexed to their wildest dreams. I run into thousands of these people everytime I go overseas.

The whole recovery programme could really do with a much better press. It's got a beaut multi taste and it'll mean a lot more jobs too, as the amounts increase and more people are required to load it on to the ships. This isn't going to help the family man, of course, or the family woman, or indeed the family children.

But the family mining investments will be all right for a while. They'll certainly be all white for a while and you can't have everything because we've sold it.

INTEREST RATES

Treasury has been under great pressure
in recent times. Too much pressure,
in my view.

Gidday. Now I'd like to have a word or two with you today about interest rates. I've been asked a fair bit lately to comment on the likelihood of their going up.

My answer to this is that I've made a policy for some years now of not indulging in quantitative speculation, and it would be inconsistent of me to start now. I know this is not an answer to the question. All I ever said was that it is *my* answer. In fact of course, I've also been asked whether or not, if there is a rise after the democracy, it'll be in the order of 1–1½ per cent.

And my answer to that is that firstly, the economic circumstances surrounding interest rate movements are very uncertain and they do contain a lot of variables and that more importantly I've got every confidence that a lot of, secondly; people will ultimately lose track of the thirdly; question and I'll be able to insinuate a new question into the response in such a way as to end up talking about fourthly; something else altogether.

It's difficult to explain how this will have any real effect on interest rates, and as I said I don't really want to talk about interest rates at all, and if you want to talk about interest rates, then I suggest you either talk about them amongst yourselves or bide your time until after the democracy, when I'll be making a full and detailed statement about them.

I know I said in 1977 that interest rates would fall, but I must remind you of the context of that remark. It wasn't supposed to have been reported at all.

It was made at the departmental Xmas party, and I've got a photograph that establishes beyond any question that the context wasn't at all well. It had a revolving bow-tie on and to the trained eye the rather substantial luminous red nose was something of a giveaway. I saw it the next morning, and it pulled up very badly indeed. Which has got nothing to do with interest rates either.

THE ENGLISH ECONOMY

The English economy has altered its status, from that of model to that of object lesson.

Gidday. Now I'd like to have a word or two with you today about the way the English economy is shaping up because the implications for the Australian economy are extremely important, and a lot of the people around the office here seem to be in some dismay about the poor showing of the monetarist approach, and of course Friedman's been claiming for some time now that Margaret's copy of the handbook has got a few pages missing and that putting the thing into practice is giving the theory a bad name.

And obviously there are grounds for considerable concern in all of this, although I don't think we should get too despondent about it. There are certain lessons to be learnt by all means, and if it becomes obvious that we should change our tack, then let's do it, but let's do it responsibly. And let's deny that we're doing it.

The first thing is that the relationship between unemployment and inflation seems to have taken issue with the Phillip's Curve, and the Keynesian assumptions were knocked down to a private collector the other day without reaching the reserve.

What's supposed to happen is that an inversely proportional movement in the variables will ensure that if you can get unemployment up to just short of calling out the army, inflation will tend to come down a bit and you can give the impression that you're actually running things. This can be laid out in the form of a graph or an equation, and if you've ever *seen* a seesaw you'll probably be pretty much at home with the principle.

The problem at the moment is that having got one end of the seesaw up, they've discovered what they think might be a design fault, and the other end not only won't come down, but now it's decided it wants an ice-cream.

This wouldn't normally bother us unduly, except that we've just signed for another couple of seasons with the same seesaw company, and the swings and slides we ordered last time were a big disappointment.

So if it's all the same with you, when the seesaws arrive, none of us speaks English, and we don't know anything about it.

THE SCHOOL-TO-WORK INITIATIVES

The government has recognised problems in Australian society. It is sometimes said that the government hasn't dealt with these problems. This is piffle.

Gidday. Now I'd like to have a word or two with you today about the 'school-to-work' initiatives we'll be introducing in the next couple of weeks. We call them initiatives because you can't very well come right out and call them a catastrophe and still expect people to get behind them and pretend they're not going to fall over coming out of the mobile barrier.

The idea itself has about it the sort of simplicity you've no doubt come to expect by now. It's based on the need to give Ian Viner something to get up and announce from time to time and I think he really did announce it pretty well. He thrives on this type of work, although we have had a little bit of trouble with the planning of precisely what the announcement should consist of.

We did already have a series of school-to-work programmes that were designed to facilitate the transition between school and work, but some difficulty was apparent in this area because in many cases the transition was fairly open-ended due to the paucity of work in the right-hand side of the equation. So we toyed with a transition period between school

33

and the period when people were looking for work, but we reacted against the negativism of this approach by planning a commencement of the benefit at 18, and trying to piece together a school-to-school programme for the others.

But this might have involved some measure of expenditure on the education budget and we rejected the idea in favour of a school-to-sleep programme. However, it seemed that the present system of education has the school-to-sleep movement fairly well in hand, and so it was that we came back to Ian Viner. And his opinion, and it's not just his opinion of course, he took advice from wherever he could without leaving the building, was that it was high time he announced something.

If that's not initiative, I'll get on to the milliner, personally, and order my lunch to be brought around on a stand.

TAXATION REFORM

The Treasury has looked at taxation reform for some time, and has decided that, in general terms, it should keep looking.

Gidday. Now I'd like to have a word or two with you today about the taxation system in this country, and the plans we've got at the moment for taxation reform are, in a nutshell, and obviously that's where we'd like to keep them for the moment. But I can discuss with you the range of options we're looking at.

The main problem is that the government needs to get hold of more revenue from somewhere, because the amount we're getting in theory hasn't actually materialised in practice. Quite a lot of people at the northern end of the income scale have apparently decided not to pay a great deal of tax, and the obvious answer is to get a bit more out of the rest of you. This is not going to be easy and I am going to need a couple of volunteers from the audience.

There are several ways of doing it. We could introduce a value added tax, which we've already denied we're going to do. We could bring in some alternative sort of retail tax, which we'd be loathe to do, because there's some suggestion that if we stack it on top of the CPI, it might block out the sun, and of course trying to reduce inflation in the dark is very specialised work indeed.

The idea of extending the wholesale tax has got a lot in its favour because it doesn't go past the top copy of the invoice, and if shopkeepers can learn to go about their normal duties with stockings pulled down over their faces, it might just work.

35

Then there's the question of a resources rental tax which we also denied we were thinking about, and I'm not saying we're thinking about it now; but I won't deny that we're thinking that perhaps the denial that we were thinking about it might have to be recalled and checked over for a minor design fault in the shockers.

So there are certainly a few options available and I'll let you know what we decide to do shortly after we've done it.

THE FUTILE BAN

People generally don't understand trade sanctions, and governments must waste valuable time explaining the enormous effect such measures can have, if used properly.

Gidday. Now I suppose you noticed, as I did, the reports of quite massive numbers of group suicides in the upper reaches of the Russian industrial sector following Malcolm's decision to stop the export of futile. Of course these export bans have come in for a fair amount of rather ill-informed criticism in recent days, and I'd like, if I may, to counter just perhaps one or two of the more outrageous charges before we go any further.

The first thing is, of course, that some people claim the Russians can get any amount of futile from South Africa. This is not true.

For this to happen, the Russians would have to offer the South Africans a certain amount of money for the futile, the South Africans would have to agree that the futile was saleable at that price, and then, in the extremely unlikely event that these complex negotiations were concluded satisfactorily, the futile would have to be loaded into some sort of ocean-going embargo and actually shipped from South Africa right across the great big ocean to Russia.

And I don't know whether you've been to the beach lately, but believe you me the sea is an extremely harsh mistress and crossing large stretches of it with futile jammed into every spare corner would be a pretty perilous business.

37

I'm not saying it's impossible, but I'm sure you can all see that it isn't really very likely.

The other thing is that I understand that certain people, whose names are being ferried to me even as I speak, claim that there's some inconsistency in our rejecting the $2 million futile contract, and yet continuing with our $300 million wool sale arrangement.

This is just silly. You can't keep a strike force in the air for hours on end with wool. If you could, our air force would have the azure pretty much at its mercy.

We've got to keep things in perspective. There's no point in sending the country broke, because if we're broke, we won't be able to pay for the war I'm challenging Russia not to start.

We've got to be humane too of course. People need clothing, particularly during wars, and warm clothing is in special demand during cold wars. Although if the war heats up, then of course we'll put wool on the embargo list with futile, and a whole lot of other things we don't produce at Nareen either.

THE FUTILE BAN
IS CALLED OFF

Even ludicrously small changes must be
reported, if the sanctions are to be seen
as successful.

Gidday. Now before I get down to a detailed explanation of the enormity of my recent achievements overseas, the medium to high-fire danger in Afghanistan and the precise date of the election, there is just one point of policy I'd like to clear up.

It's only a very minor point, and reasons for the very slight alteration in our national stance are obvious enough; but even very small and extremely insignificant very minor un-important little matters of no particular moment in any conventionally accepted sense of the word do need clearing up every now and again when, for some reason or another, some barely perceptible alteration is effected in the appearance of an aspect of the total very minor point as a whole.

The ban on the export of futile to the single U double S single R has been lifted, actually by the cabinet, and to that extent it has been called off, cancelled, reversed and moved into a standing-on-its-head profit situation.

The reasons, as I say, are obvious enough, but on the off-chance that there's someone out there who doesn't recognise the tell-tale signs of a passionate concern for truth, moral rectitude, consistency and an upturn in the June quarter, I'll just run very quickly through the reasons.

The futile was initially banned because it was felt the purchaser could use it as a component in the war effort of the relentless southern thrust of the red catastrophe. Since then, several arguments of an extremely persuasive nature have been put to me.

Firstly, if we don't sell it to them, someone else will, which is a moral point.

Secondly, if we don't sell it to them, there's no guarantee that we won't really be selling it to them under a false name in egg cartons, which is another moral point.

Thirdly, futile isn't really of any use whatsoever in the Russian military effort so feared by the people who have been watching me do Richard III in the last few weeks. Futile can be used to make bombs of course, as we said when we banned it, but the bombs aren't strategic, and there's some suggestion that they don't even hurt.

And in the face of this moral barrage, we have decided to flag the $200 away and try for the fridge.

MORE ABOUT SANCTIONS

If the public consistently refuses to
understand the effectiveness of sanctions,
the issue must be spelt out in simple terms.

Gidday. Now I've noticed in the tissues in recent days a disturbing tendency to question the consistency of what I have every reason to believe is our policy on the hounding of the Afghans.

Let me say once again, as I repeated in a reiteration made last week, and reported fairly widely, that our response to the events which have taken place in the Middle-East-flashpoint-region has been measured and responsible. And to be more specific it's measured in votes and responsible to Washington.

This has involved us in taking a good strong stand, and then maintaining it in the face of movements in and around the general area of money. Which has been seen in certain fairly predictable circles as being perhaps some slight evidence for a very faint element of inconsistency.

This is quite wrong. In fact, of course, it represents the one entirely consistent aspect in everything we've done.

There's no point in refusing to sell to the Russians things they'd be able to buy from someone else. What we're trying to do here is not merely to make some grand moral gesture. We're trying, as we always have been, to make some fairly grand amount of money.

If we refuse to sell wool, we can reasonably expect the Russians to decide that rather than freeze to death, they should perhaps make some attempt to ship something in from some other slightly less principled nation. Likewise, if we refuse to sell futile, we must recognise the possibility that they'll get it from someone else.

If we say we're not going to sell them uranium or H-bombs or tanks or explosives or flame-throwers, we're only standing in the way of our own well-being. We've got to ban the sale only of items they can't get from anywhere else at all, and which will therefore frustrate them as a nation and embarrass and confound their leaders.

And to this end I hereby ban the sale to Russia of the Sullivans, King's Kitchen, the Young Dickiebirds and Unhinged Foreign Policy.

SANCTIONS AND WOOL

When the policy of trade sanctions is thought to be jeopardised by individual behavioral tendencies, stern words are sometimes instructive.

Gidday. Now I'd like to have a word or two with you about the dangerous insinuations being bruited about in the clubs of our major cities that I have been involved in some way, to a greater or lesser extent, in selling wool to the Russians.

This is patently absurd. It stands in direct contravention of everything I've been saying. Well, perhaps not direct contravention, but it certainly doesn't rest at all easily with the spirit of what I've been saying. Well, perhaps that's not as unimpeachable as it might be either, but I think we can say that the allegations do seem to be not entirely consistent with certain parts of some of the things I've been attempting to outline for you.

In other words, I never said I wouldn't. After all, the business of this country is business, and someone's got to mind the store while we all discuss the morality of storeminding.

Nevertheless, the thing that concerns me most is the suggestion that the brands were changed on the actual bales from Daggeen.

Let me say that if this happened at all, it certainly wasn't at my instigation. Someone's made a decision for reasons unknown to me personally, and I'm not my keeper's brother, and in fact the running of Daggeen tends perforce to tick over without my steadying hand for substantial periods. But if the brands were changed, I think I say without fear of bankruptcy, that the intention was not to sneak the Daggeen wool-clip off up the Volga under an unassuming name in a cynical attempt to pull down a rapid ruble in these parlous times.

The idea would have been, if I might interpret the actions of others in doing something I'm not even sure happened, to protect my produce from the wilful stupidity of certain unnamed organisations who might refuse to load it because they don't like me.

That's the state we've reached in this country. A man has to refuse to sell his wool under a different name in order to fail to make a decent return on capital.

I don't know what things are coming to. Although I've got a fair idea where they're going.

WHITHER SANCTIONS?

Once trade sanctions have succeeded in one case, they can be applied with confidence wherever they are needed.

Gidday. Now I'd like to have a word or two with you today about the wonderful kaleidoscopic world of trade sanctions.

I know a lot of people don't really understand exactly what's going on in this area, and I feel I should take the opportunity to come out with a full run-down of precisely what we're doing, and why we're thinking of doing it.

As you may know, in an effort to orchestrate a concerted response to Iran, the Americans have asked their allies to put their money some considerable distance from their mouths and impose trade sanctions. And the action taken by the EEC nations has fallen somewhat short of the total trade ban requested.

But in keeping with Australia's established role in the vanguard of total confusion, we've taken the lead in the matter, and have complied with the requirement almost to the letter. We've come out virtually on our own by imposing trade on Iran. We've then looked at the trade in some detail, and we've sanctioned it.

The actual wording of our trade embargo, which incidentally leaves first thing tomorrow morning if you'd like to whip down and help with some of the heavy lifting, was absolutely unequivocal. We resolved to call for an embargo of 'all items, commodities and products'. We were going to include 'things' but it seemed a little too constricting, so we dropped it back to just 'all items, commodities and products; except food, medicine and supplies intended strictly for medical purposes'. And of course the two crucial words in immediate juxtaposition there are 'except' and 'food'.

The Australian government believes that it is in the interest of all countries to bring home to the Iranians food and medical supplies, to indicate that their behaviour is rejected by the international community. Except food, of course, and supplies intended strictly for medical purposes.

SANCTIONS PROVE THEMSELVES

If there is any doubt that trade sanctions are effective, the trade figures themselves can sometimes swing open the door to understanding.

Gidday. Now I don't know whether or not you noticed this the other day, but our trade figures with Russia for the nine months to March have been released, and if you can't keep your feet still as I read you the edited highlights, don't worry about it. Just let yourselves go. You can dance out in the middle as soon as we shift the chairs back. Everyone pick a partner and just form yourselves into little coalitions wherever you can. You're only young once. Go for your lives.

I've had these figures presented to me in the form of a comparison with the corresponding period for 1979. You'll see how it works as we go along.

Barley for example, $48 million, up from 0 the year before, which is a pretty spectacular performance. Incidentally, not one grain of the 1979 tonnage was used by military or civil authorities in the unpalatably communist state, and the $48 million 1980 shipment was smuggled into the country by the marquis, and was fed in only very limited amounts to dying dissidents, critical of the Soviet aspirations in Afghania.

Wool, up $50 million to about $180 million.

Wheat, up $250 million, and this has got nothing to do with America's disappearance from the market place. We are not making up an American shortfall here. We attribute the increase to better packaging and a superior thrust at wholesale level.

American Shortfall, up $5 million to $347 million.

Sanctions, a phenomenal $312 million improvement, not including Boycotts, which showed an improvement of a billion and a half on their own.

Futile, a 15 per cent upturn.

Effective Boycotts. As you know, unfortunately this line was discontinued, as it was felt it might have been a little too specific.

Biggest Threat To World Peace Since World War II, an improvement of $63 million. An overall increase of a million zillion dollars a day.

I know there'll be people who see some miniscule tendency in all this, for personal and national greed, and personal and national hypocrisy. And I'll tell you now that all joking aside, if we don't sell things, we'll be poor. And I have to say that I find that a shameful position to be in.

DOG EAT SANCTIONS

The disadvantages of trade sanctions are minimal, and with proper understanding they could be eliminated.

Gidday. Now I'd like to have a word or two with you about the American government's rather curious attitude to wheat sales.

You might remember something about the beginning of this. The United States government decided, in order to press home the point about truth, justice and the Afghan way of life, to cut back their wheat exports to Russia to 8 million tonnes. Which is not a lot of wheat.

I know it sounds like a lot of wheat, and I've seen a photograph of some of it and it certainly looks like a lot of wheat, but apparently it has been trained to look like that by the American State Department, and in fact it's not a lot of wheat at all.

We slipped into line with the principle of not a lot of wheat by reducing our own exports to 3·9 million tonnes. Well, 'reducing' is probably not really the most accurate reflection of what we did. In fact, of course, we increased our exports to 3·9 million tonnes.

But having got them up there, we certainly refused to increase them any further, and this is what we called a 'wheat embargo'. Rightly or wrongly. We had to give it a name for the in-house newsletter, and we called it a 'wheat embargo'.

Now by pegging our exports back to the highest in history, we were supporting the Americans, to the extent that we weren't supplying the Russians with wheat they'd otherwise have bought in 5th Avenue.

We were specifically asked not to make up an American shortfall, and we didn't.

And I'm delighted to report to you that the Americans are coming out of the wheat surplus they've been experiencing since that time by getting hold of their shortfall and dumping it in China. And I really don't want to seem too churlish about this, but the Chinese are our best wheat market at the moment, and I don't see why our wonderful allies are going in there, over the top of us, without a bit of a pre-Xmas drink and a natter.

There must have been some mistake. And I've got a nasty feeling I might have been there when I made it.

SANCTIONS ARE OFF

The principles governing trade sanctions cannot be re-stated too often or too well.

Gidday. Now I'd like to have a word or two with you today about the lifting of our trade embargo on Iran. I outlined how this breathtakingly vigorous measure worked when I talked about the imposition of it. You might remember I came on between the pantomime-horse and the team of jugglers from the Wheat Board.

So I don't intend going right back over it again. The main point is that it had in common with all our other embargoes, the fact that it wasn't really an embargo. It was a partial embargo. We refused point-blank to sell them all the things they didn't want a lot of anyway, and we imposed upon them increased quantities of some of the things we thought, for humanitarian reasons, we could make a fortune out of.

The principal departure from normal business practice was that because the embargo was in operation, we filed the money under 'E'. Actually we re-labelled a lot of the files until we had twenty-five 'E's', and a big box under the desk marked 'C' for the Country Party. It filled up shortly after we imposed the biggest wheat export ever seen on the Russians, who are morally unsound, of course, but pretty sensible on matters of food intake.

As far as the Iranian embargo is concerned, now that the Americans have come up with the return fare for the hostages by giving Iran a few billion dollars that belonged to Iran, we've decided to open the booster-valve again and see what this thing will do on the open road.

I think the Iranians have learned a fairly valuable lesson about Australia. We're not prepared to stand about and do nothing while human rights are openly violated. If we are going to stand about, we'll make a few bob while we're doing it.

THE LABOR PARTY: MARCH 1980

The Labor Party normally begins an election campaign very strongly, despite anything you might hear to the contrary.

Gidday. Now I'd like to have a word with you about the quite disturbing amount of criticism levelled in recent times at the Labor Party, because I think that not only is it unfair, it's not really very well-informed.

And I think we've got to take some of the blame for this. Perhaps we could have done more in the publicity line. Perhaps more could have been said about what we've been doing. Perhaps not enough is known about what the party's thinking and where the party's going, or where the party thinks it's going or where the party's thinking has gone and who saw it last. And I want to remedy this, so let's have a look at what's going on.

The Prime Minister, as everyone knows, has made a fairly extensive fool of himself with all this baying about the Russians. And our attitude to this question was made a matter of public record in very few uncertain terms. We said, quite clearly, that had we been in government, we'd have given very serious consideration to baying a little bit less and perhaps baying a little earlier. We made no bones about this and unlike myself I think it's fairly widely recognised.

But more importantly, while the Liberals made fools of themselves overseas, costing the country many potatoes in air-fares and business lunches, the Labor Party took the opportunity to capitalise, by tearing itself apart in Queensland.

We hogged the headlines for days at a time when the Liberals wanted desperately to be seen as resolute and completely unified. Then when industrial unrest began to cripple the economy and it became obvious that the government was completely incapable of providing a stable and reasonable backdrop for the business of Australia, we tore ourselves to pieces again in Queensland, totally eclipsing the government's media coverage when they needed urgently to be seen as conciliatory and concerned for the welfare of others.

After all, the business of opposition is to oppose, and I don't really think anyone can say we haven't done that. Well, maybe a few in the branches, but we'll get them.

ROBERT AND WILLIAM

It is sometimes said the top end of the
Australian Labor Party is not always in
accordance with itself on the vexed
matter of captaincy.

Gidday. Now I'd like to have a word or two with you
today about precisely where Bill Hayden and I stand on the
question of where we stand with relation to the stance
assumed by either one of us with regard to standing anywhere
within a bull's roar of the stance of the other. And we're
united in this, Bill and I.

I know I've spoken about this before. But Bill and I have had our heads together since then and we've had a bit of a chin-wag about the way things are going, and we've indicated by a show of hands that it was high time an official statement was made.

I appreciate that there's a body of opinion in the media that Bill and I communicate only through our seconds and that a concerted campaign could drive a Number 9 iron right up the middle of the party and the Visigoths would get home again by about ten lengths.

This is not going to happen. We've seen this one coming and we're simply not going to fall for it.

Bill Hayden is an excellent leader. And more importantly, he is a man of immense parliamentary experience dating back, of course, to the Whitlam ministries. In fact he's one of the few people left from the Whitlam era and I think this is a point many people forget. Bill Hayden's political career is inextricably linked with the Whitlam era and not only do I respect this, I think everyone else ought to respect it too.

On top of the quite staggering political acumen he might have picked up during the Whitlam era, Bill Hayden is principally recognised as a man of considerable economic skill, and despite the so-called rift between us with regard to wages policy, I must say that over all, I'd have to say that in general terms Bill has a pretty solid grasp of economics.

I reckon he's not a bad leader. I can think of a lot worse. And I'm sorry if I've ever given the impression of not being as fulsome as I might have been in my support of him.

Of course I support Bill Hayden. Somebody's got to. And it's pretty obvious that the public has side-stepped its obligation completely.

WILLIAM AND ROBERT

Statements are sometimes required from
both sides, cards are placed on tables,
petty differences are set aside, and issues
are confronted.

Gidday. Now I'd like, if I may, to address a few remarks
to the question of my relationship with Bob Hawke.

A lot of people have been asking about this and by and
large they seem to have been asking Bob about it.

Of course, as is well-known by now, Bob and I got together
recently in the office of an approved counsellor in marriage
guidance, who incidentally isn't in favour of a 35-hour-week
either, and we talked our way through the problems the
media insists we've been having; and in fact Bob's explained

in broad outline the position as he sees the parts of it that he decided were important.

But let me say, above and beyond the remarks of the honourable member for the desperately tricky seat of Wills, that the public must understand how the party works.

Certainly Bob Hawke is a man of considerable accomplishment. Certainly he's a man of remarkable achievement in industrial relations. And there can be little doubt that the people of Australia expect that Bob Hawke will one day become Prime Minister.

But after all, this is a democracy, and what the people want is entirely academic.

I believe that with a figure of Bob Hawke's stature and capability making a contribution inside the parliamentary Labor Party, we'll be a very awesome team. And, of course, we'll be the team that has, as the under-secretary-for-scrapping-on-the-shop-floor, the man who most people feel ought to be Prime Minister.

It's been said that after the next election the party will re-assess the question of leadership and review the whole business of the front-bench line up. And I'd like to make the point that the main thing at the moment is not to be drawn into speculation about what's going to happen after the election; the main thing is the election itself, and how we're going to win it. And win it we will, if we can get the people of this country to vote for the party that *contains* the man they want to see as Prime Minister.

Although if we do win, it'll be pretty clear to me whose leadership swung the issue.

GOUGH AND ROBERT

Ex-Labor Prime Ministers make occasional
statements in the interests of solidarity.

Gidday. Now I don't want to cause any sort of rift in the
Labor Party, whose internal loyalty has been perhaps the one
great constant in Australian politics of the modern era.
Neither do I want to appear too polemical at a time when the
book-launching circuit has imbued me with a certain mellow
detachment which I must say rather appeals to me.

But on the other hand, I think it behoves me, as something
of a figurehead, to make just one or two general comments
about what's going on.

Firstly, let me say that I don't think for a moment that Bob
Hawke will be the leader of the Labor Party. Or at least he
won't be the leader of the Labor Party for some years yet.
And if he does become leader, I don't think he'll be a very good
one. Although if he isn't a very good one, history tells us he
probably will be the leader.

Hayden's the boy for me. The business of opposition is to
oppose, and Bill has now got a very solid team behind him and
he's opposing with such skill and determination I think he's
capable of leading the party into opposition again at pretty
well any tick of the clock.

I know what the opinion polls are saying, but anyone can
be popular when there's nothing much at stake. Bob isn't
even in the front line yet. There are people in the parliamentary
Labor Party right now, young people with great experience,
people like . . . well, they know who they are.

59

I don't think there's any need to assume that Bob's just going to go in there and rattle straight through the ranks, and I don't much like the campaign to garner so much public support for Hawke that when he does go in, people will come down with the vapours if he isn't stuck straight in the driver's seat.

I don't believe he'll be the leader. I don't believe he'll be the leader for a long time, and by then he'll be too old.

I think we should go with a proven leader, a leader whose appeal to the electorate is well-known. But as I say, I think Bill Hayden should remain as leader.

I don't think Bob should get the job. I don't even regard him as a possibility, and even if he were, I wouldn't want him to be the leader. We've got a leader, and I just hope Bob realises that the only person who thinks he might eventually get the job is the public of Australia.

THE QUEENSLAND ABORTION DEBATE

There can have been few more impressive demonstrations of considered and rational discourse, than the abortion debate in something called the Queensland Parliament.

Gidday. Now I'm given to understand that there have been rumours flying about the place to the effect that the ship of the Sunshine State hasn't been answering the helm in the last week or so, and that this has somehow thrown the question of my continued captaincy open for general discussion.

I know a lot of people would like nothing more than to see me sufficiently embarrassed over this business that I'd have to resign. But I can tell you now that this isn't going to happen.

Of course there may well be resignations. I've been asking for them for months, and sooner or later it's going to dawn on a few of the poltroons I work with up here that either they resign, or I'll have them classified by the National Trust and pushed over during the night.

The number of times they've changed hats in the course of the abortion debate is quite staggering. I was told everyone agreed with the legislation in the first place, but when it came to a vote, which is an idea I'm not crazy about either, people started running in all directions and we had to take the bill out the back for a while and bring it in again as an amendment to the State Drainage Act, which I thought they might at least block-vote on. But by then the notion of conscience had been introduced and we had to haul it back as a private member's bill.

The important thing is not that most people in the parliament might not want the bill passed, or that the majority of the public were against it from the kick-off. The important thing is that the government stays in power. Because if the government were removed by popular demand, the very guts of the democratic system would be eaten away. The whole place would fall to anarchy.

The people have got to be told that if they want to express their views to the State Government, and have those views reflected in legislation, then the proper thing for them to do is to move to some state where this sort of garbage is tolerated.

MALCOLM AND ERIC

Departures from the Coalition ministries
are extremely unusual. There were well
under a thousand of them in the
government's first two years in office.

Gidday. Now look, about this new cabinet of ours. It has been suggested in some of the more childish pockets of the tedia that Eric Robinson's more or less overnight departure from the batting order was forced on us by pressure from the Country Party.

This is completely unrealistic. This is not the way things work at all.

We looked very carefully at the cabinet and in line with where we thought Eric's abilities lay, we offered to shift him from the finance portfolio and arrange for his appointment as an under-secretary in the junior ministry of comparative oblivion.

For reasons best known to himself, Eric decided not to take on this responsibility. He decided instead to throw a bit of extra effort into his Reg Withers impression in the lower house and I'd like to wish him all the best with this but I'm not going to, and I think Eric will be among the very first to understand why. Reg will be first, of course, but I don't think Eric will be very far from the leading bunch, and with any luck the leading bunch won't lose too much contact with who's supposed to be actually running things around here.

Shuffling a cabinet is not an easy thing to do, of course, and obviously fingers will be burnt, or hands and arms, or heads or whatever the Country Party slaps a demolition order on. But there are other considerations as well.

We've got to include people from the states on a roughly proportional basis; we've got to include some senators, although we've decided since 1978 to do this on an alphabetical basis and I'm afraid the bulk of glamour work has gone well before the W's swing into view.

All in all, I think we've come out of it fairly well, although if there's any trouble from the back benches during the current term, let the Country Party sort it out. They got me into this.

THE DUNSTAN REPORT

For hundreds of years, people have written
about worms. 1980 saw a turnaround.

Gidday. Now I don't want to get too silly about this, but
some rather disturbing facts have come to light as a result of
this report. And if I might make an attempt, for the sake of
brevity, to synthesise what I see as the more essential elements
of it, I'd have to say the most worrying single aspect is the
quite remarkable discovery that Don Dunstan did in fact
have an actual private life.

It's quite clear from even the most cursory appraisal of the report that when Don Dunstan had completed his day's work as Premier, he went home. It has even been suggested, although I'm bound to say this isn't actually spelt out in the report, that when he got home he sometimes had a meal. 'Dinner', he called it, according to Mr Iscariot who appears to have had some sort of advances made to him by a publishing company.

And as I say, I don't want to get too hysterical about this, but the possibility that at some stage after the prandials Don slipped into his PJ's and went to bed simply can't be ruled out. And the implication that he went to sleep from time to time, possibly during what the report refers to as 'nighnigh's', is obviously there if you care to look for it.

The report itself is completely lacking in any sort of partiality of course. This goes without saying. Nothing else does, but I don't think there's any real question that this does. It was independently commissioned. I know this to be the case because I commissioned it myself and I remember being in a decidedly independent frame of mind at the time.

And the timing of its release has got nothing to do with the federal election. I was asked to release it by a bloke I ran into in a shaving mirror. But anyway, I think the public has a right to know. I think they want to know. I think they can reasonably expect to be told these things, and as long as I'm in charge around here they can certainly expect to be told what I want them to think they know.

And if you'd like a copy of the report or any of the other publications we do up here, 'The Famous 5 and the Big Spookie House', 'Bill McMahon on $5 per day', just drop us a line. Any line. Someone's bound to fall for it.

THE COST OF LABOR POLICIES

During an election campaign, a sense of proportion is extremely valuable.

Gidday. Now I'd like to have a word or two with you today about the cost of some of the Labor Party's election promises; I mentioned this in the House the other day but there was an exhibition of community singing going on and I'm not convinced that my remarks were fully appreciated.

But it is important, because election promises do have to be paid for and you know as well as I do that most people in this country can't afford to pay for anything.

So let's look at what they're proposing. Firstly, there's the health programme. Our estimates of the cost of this indicate an overall increase of $476000 million, or in other words, $893527 million billion.

If you come over here and look at that through this little viewfinder, you'll see that . . . hang on a minute, it's gone behind a tree. There it is now, just adjust the focus again and you'll see for yourselves that it's really $991 748 million billion zillion, and I don't want to bother you but there's a tertiary assistance scheme out there somewhere that's going to cost $11 500 million; and I don't know whether or not you know what that sort of money costs but we estimate that you're not going to get out of it under $100 000 billion a month.

The real worry is the employment programme which our figures indicate is going to cost $1625 million billion zillion a day just in interest payments, and you're looking at an all-up figure of $200 000 billion zillion umptillion and what inflation will do to that after the first year is anyone's guess. According to our figures inflation will be about 17 000 per cent, the CPI will be up over the storm water drains and one and one will be 688 million 790 622 billion.

I hope you're taking a few notes here. New maths is going to be very important in the next few weeks.

THE DEMOCRATS

The possibility that a third party might
hold the balance of power, is one that
calls for desperate measures.

Gidday. Now I'd like to have a word or two with you today about the Senate, because if I play my cards right control-above-stairs might turn out to be the major election issue. I know it's not a real election issue, but it is an issue and it has got something to do with the election.

And more importantly of course, the Liberal Party sees it as an election issue and it's no coincidence that they're prepared to spend $100000 million billion to keep us from holding the balance of power.

Our position on all of this has been stated several times and it has tended to vary with atmospheric conditions and the way I felt at the time and the statements of other people's positions and the audience response and the date and the way things seemed to be going and the facts as they came to hand and our comparative good fortune with the barrier draw; and I would say to any donkeys out there, you won't regret it, it's a wise decision you won't be making and we'll certainly be doing your very best for us.

While I've got you here, just a quick word about Malcolm. I said a couple of weeks ago that he was a friendless and joyless man, and I said last week that he was a man of brilliant intellectual capacity and a brilliant politician and that he was sincere and honest in his foreign policies.

69

This is not precisely the sort of cowering and fawning I object to so strongly in the other parties. This is the fearless voice of the completely independent strong man of Australia's public life.

We do have a policy. I don't have it with me at the moment, it's in my other trousers.

But I can tell you that our general aim in the Senate is to keep the Government honest, and whether or not we're able to do this will depend largely on whether we're going for the short donkey-ride or the more fabled affair with the palm leaves.

ROBERT MISQUOTED

Hawke the Staunch Denies US Reports of Disloyalty

Age, 30 June 1980

Gidday. Now I'd like to depart slightly from accepted practice today and I'll try to do this as briefly as possible. I know a lot of you have other functions to go to.

Just one point really. These remarks I made in America. Firstly I didn't make them, secondly I didn't make them in America, and thirdly they weren't reported correctly.

In fact I'm not really sure where this story came from, but there are two elements of it I think I should comment on. I don't think we'll lose the next election. I'm not even sure we lost the last one. I think we're going to put up a performance that'll surprise a lot of people. I certainly don't see any point in going into an election believing you can't win it, and I see no mileage at all in *saying* you aren't going to win it.

But it's the other point that really annoys me. It's been suggested by the conspiracy of ignorance that seems to have the run of the media in this place, and I exclude Rupert from this specifically. I think he knows what's going on and I don't think he's going to run away from it if the cock crows all afternoon.

It's been suggested by these people that Bill Hayden's going to stand down if we lose the election. Now obviously there's very little to be gained from spending too much time on the hypothetical. Anything might happen.

But in this case I think there is some value in it, because even without knowing what's going to happen in the election, I can tell you that if we lose it, Bill will not be standing down in favour of me.

And the reason I'm able to state this with such conviction is that that would be a sensible and fair thing to do. It would be quite reasonable to let him have one last all-out attempt and then if it doesn't work, let him stand aside and be replaced by someone else.

This is a bit too rational for the Labor Party, or the Opposition as it's come to be known. And if ever I did float the idea of having the party led by the most popular person in the country, it certainly wouldn't be with any hope that it might happen.

THE QUEENSLAND SENATE TICKET

There was unfavourable comment from certain sections of the media, when the Queensland Premier announced that the number one position on the Senate ticket was to be taken by his wife.

Gidday. Now I'd like to make a couple of points about the way things work in this district. I had a bloke in here this morning with a photograph of a rather imposing looking woman sitting on the bonnet of one of the early Austins at what appeared to be some manner of staff picnic.

I had never seen this woman before. She didn't even remind me of anyone. I certainly didn't recognise the background, and I have no recollection of ever having seen any photograph at home that looked anything like it.

The main point is that the woman is definitely not my grandfather's younger sister. And even if she were, and even if this character could prove that he was her grandson, that would still not necessarily mean that he could go into the Senate unopposed.

This place is after all a demongratule and it works along quite well recognised demongratorial lines. You can't just come in here with your photograph album and a partly-drafted drainage bill and expect to be lofted straight into some sort of Darwinian holding pattern.

The ultimate decision about the make up of the State Government is expressed through the ballot-box, and this is done by secret ballot. And if we're going to have a secret ballot, it can't really come as a great surprise that we keep the ballot-box in a secret place.

Now in case anything happens to me, and I don't know whether or not you've ever seen a stress fracture but it isn't always attractive, I have vouchsafed the exact position of the ballot box to my next of con and at this stage that's as far as we want to take it, and if the State doesn't make a pretty remarkable saving by having the bi-annual cabinet meeting in the second bedroom, I'll eat my hat subsidy. There will be criticism of course, but you can't have everything, unless there are two of you, in which case you can have half of everything each.

THE OBJECTIVE PRESS

For the first time in many years, a major daily newspaper stated publicly that it would not tell its readers how to vote in a national election.

Gidday. Now I'd like to have a word or two with you today about our newspaper coverage of the election because, as you'll no doubt be acutely aware, we took the unprecedented step of not telling you how to vote, and on the whole I must say I think the coverage benefited from the balanced line we were able to chart during the campaign.

Of course there were doubters. Some people said that to abstain from stating a position in the argument was to lend support to the status quo, but this doesn't add up because I'm not going to discuss it.

The main thing I want to talk about is not what we chose to do, but how we chose to do it, and this is where I think we did particularly well.

By standing aside from the hectoring and band-wagoning that went on in the body of the press, we were able to make a proper assessment of the issues as we saw them, and consequently, of course, of the issues as you saw them. We were able to look in a much more considered and detached way at the differences between the policies offered by the Liberals and the Socialists, and we were in an excellent position to discuss the very worrying trend in the polls leading up to Saturday.

Our analysis of the economic consequences of the Socialist platform was able to be conducted completely without any sort of bias whatever, and we were prevented from going into too much detail about the social concerns of the nation by avowedly not siding with the party which cares about such things.

I really think the whole thing went pretty well and I'm certainly in favour of the principle of non-alignment, and I'm absolutely committed to the *statement* of the principle of non-alignment, certainly during an election. It doesn't matter so much the rest of the time.

THE DAGG POLL

Labor Comfortably in Lead, Poll Shows
Age, 15 October 1980

Labor Still Ahead: Poll
Age, 17 October 1980

Libs Defy the Polls
Age, 20 October 1980

Gidday. Now I'd like to have a word or two with you today about the opinion polls, and more particularly, of course, about the Dagg Poll which was released on the Thursday before the election and indicated that the Labor Party would get in by about 165 seats.

Certainly this didn't happen, although in all fairness it should be pointed out that we didn't say it would happen. What we said was that if a general election had been held a fortnight earlier in the back bar of the Imperial in Manangatang, the swing would have been such as to compel the coalition to go out and spend about a zillion dollars on advertising in the last week and get back in by something in the region of about 23 seats.

That's what the poll said if you read it the right way, and the right way to read a poll is about a month afterwards.

Of course the big thing about the polls this year was that they indicated a swing to Labor. And a swing to Labor is exactly what presented itself on the big day.

There was some suggestion that the swing wasn't even. This is quite true. We didn't say it would be. We didn't say it wouldn't be either. We didn't say anything about it, except that there would be one if the early figures were anything to go by.

In defence of our attitude I would just make the point that swings do tend to be uneven. And if people are going to go around assuming that swings are going to be even simply because no one suggests that they probably won't be, then obviously some of the more hysterical extrapolaters are going to get a big surprise when the swing to Labor turns out to be colossal where it isn't needed and slightly inadequate in some of the more crucial litmus cliffhangers.

The other worry with polls is that people might sometimes say they're going to do something and then when the pressure's on they might do something else. This is called a broken promise, and of course the air's so thick with them around election time it's difficult to know what's going on.

But I make no apologies for our performance at all. Money yes, but I draw the line at apologies.

ECONOMISTS AND THE ELECTION

Many people wonder why election night telecasts are so dependably uninteresting.

Gidday. Now a lot of people have asked about our election coverage, both in the run-up to the democracy, and in the nerve-centre-tally-pulse-computer room as the scores came in from our around-the-grounds personnel and were analysed by being repeated until new ones came in.

And the particular point raised in most of the inquiries was that the discussion of the campaigns tended to be conducted by economists.

I don't deny this. We had a team of economic analysts working for us throughout the campaign and their comments were run in both the printed and electronic media. Although I would make the point that we did have a couple of non-economists in the mix, and their remarks were designed to be seen as a more general coverage. About economics certainly, but a much more general coverage.

I would say that the reason for the emphasis on economics was that the axiomatic element in the election was economics. We decided this considerably in advance of the election itself, and having hired so many economists, there didn't seem any real value in straying very far from economics as a central theme.

It's been suggested that there might have been some discussion about social policies and one or two of the things that might have had some importance to the voters. And in all fairness I think we tried to do this.

We costed all the policies and we looked very closely at the effect they might be expected to have on interest rates and taxation and various other indices that are quite readily understood by economists.

We wanted to look in some detail at things like health and the problems of the unemployed, but the only economist we knew who was sick couldn't come in due to illness, and unfortunately none of the celebrities we have on our books at the moment is unemployed; although we did talk about unemployment as a componential variable in the Greedmanist equation, and if the English economy doesn't get a bit more healthy than it looked in the Liberal Party's ads, Greedman himself could be unemployed pretty well any day now.

But if our emphasis on economics did nothing else, at least it explains why no one else was very interested, and it goes some way to explaining why we had no idea at all about what the electorate was thinking.

THE HIDDEN UNEMPLOYED

Even during a rigorous election campaign,
the government must ensure that the
economy is working.

Gidday. Now I don't know whether or not you noticed this in the run up to the cliffhanger, but some new unemployment figures were released last week, and if you thought unemployment was high beforehand, you might like to just grab your hat and go for a little stroll while the rest of us go through this for spelling mistakes.

The reason that the new figures are a bit more lofty than the style to which we've become accustomed is that someone has included some of the unemployed in the calculations.

The unemployed who have been included this time are called the 'hidden unemployed', which means they're the same as the rest of the unemployed in that they're unemployed, but they've been hidden from us by not having been mentioned in unemployment figures. And if you're not going to mention the unemployed in unemployment figures, it's highly unlikely that they're going to show up anywhere else, unless they go overseas and are somehow recorded as invisible exports.

But the main thing about them is that there are half a million of them, and if they're added to the other group of *un*-hidden unemployed, we're looking at about 900 000 although, of course, you can't see the whole group because 500 000 of them are hidden behind things.

But let's make no mistake about the country. The country is lucky. I don't know whether you've ever seen it from the air, but the higher you get the luckier it looks, and this applies on the ground as well, of course.

I must admit I was very surprised about the 500 000 hidden unemployed. It hadn't occurred to me that some people are sufficiently disheartened to just give up and not even register as unemployed.

This is a big surprise to me. I had no idea about this, and none of the other people around here have had any idea for a long time, which might be part of the problem, although I do wish someone had hidden it better.

MALCOLM AND JOHN

In January 1981, Sir John Kerr returned
to the scene of his Governor-Generalship.

Gidday. Now I'd like to clarify the remarks I made the other day about Surgeon Kerr, and I realise this is an emotional issue for a lot of people, but there can surely be little doubt that the surgeon has paid a very high price indeed for the action he took in dismissing the government the press had already destroyed.

I had lunch with him recently, and the price he paid for that was fair and reasonable I thought, but it wasn't an official lunch because the surgeon doesn't have an official capacity these days. We've got a rough idea of what he can function on, but a proper medical estimate hasn't been available for some time.

But I want to clear something up about what I said afterwards. I said, 'he has paid a very very high price'. I did not say, as I saw suggested somewhere, that he *was* paid a very very high price. He wasn't. He wasn't paid anything. We had to withdraw the job offer we had made out in his name, and he's been getting by in the meantime on the ex-title-holder's allowance, which is considerably short of the King's Ransom he was popularly supposed to have received.

More importantly, I'd like to mention his privately declared intention of coming back here as a non-assisted migrant. There's been some hint in the press that he's probably done his time in solitary, and that basically what he did in the first place wasn't his idea anyway.

And I'd just like to say that it was. He might have been led astray by the crowd he was running with at the time, but it was his decision and the crowd he'd been running with before he ran across us was not the sort of crowd that would do him any good.

The action he took was entirely his own, and I don't want anyone thinking that he was influenced in any way by the fact that we told him to do it and nailed the place to the ground until he did.

If anyone's to blame, and I'm not suggesting for a moment that anyone is, it certainly isn't me. I was over at the sheriff's place that night playing euchre with the vicar's sister, a traveller in bicycles and a bloke who kept telling me he was the Chief Justice.

CHARLES AS A G-G

The question of a new Governor-General has occupied the nation for some time.

Gidday. Now I suppose you all heard the other night the piteous racket put up by Bill Hayden about the prospect of having His Enormity come out here as some sort of Governor General. And if ever a dismal, hopeless, uncharitable, down-in-the-boots attitude were required for open public display, here it most certainly is in the grey corner.

I might say that Bill Hayden has never struck me as a man particularly given to pageantry, and it's hardly surprising really, I suppose, that here he is to be found once more, lurking in the shadows with his blanket and his little watering can and a lot of fatuous nationalistic poppycock about appointing an Australian.

Now don't get me wrong here. I'm certainly not coming out against Australians. They're wonderful people and clearly there's a place for them in many areas of the public life. There are some in Telecom.

But this job really is one out of the box. The requirement is after all for someone to represent the English monarch, and whether you like it or not there can't be a lot of people better equipped to do this type of work than the monarch's own son. That's really not bad as representing goes.

Aside from anything else, of course, if you accept the idea of a foreign monarch's having an overseer out here, as a completely independent observer of how people react to having the government sacked, it surely doesn't much matter who it is.

I think Bill's misjudged the mood of the people on this one. And I think if he hasn't, we can probably shift the mood of the people around a bit until he has.

Of course it's still only a suggestion at this stage. We'll have to see how things go, and of course this sort of appointment isn't a thing that'll be decided by the flip of a coin.

I'm not sure quite what method Royalty uses to make up its mind, but if we are to be blessed by the Presence, someone had better have a pretty serious natter with Bill.

THE ELLICOTT APPOINTMENT

The idea that a Liberal Minister could resign and be appointed to the High Court, drew comment from the Labor Party.

Gidday. Now between ourselves the Labor Party has been spotted again recently. I don't know whether or not we've got a precise fix on its exact position, and I'm not sure that *it's* got any genuine understanding of its position at the moment. But it's apparently been seen somewhere and I must say it's nice to have it up and about again.

We had a message in here that it took a pretty dim view of the most recent appointment to the Federal Court. The idea of appointing a political figure to the bench was not under serious threat, but there seemed to be some dismay at the particular appointment permitted by the non-objectionable system.

I imagine that the acquiescence in the matter of the system is largely to do with the expectation that when the Labor Party gets into power, and any century now they'll give it an awful surprise, they'll be able to load the Federal Court and other similar bodies with some of the many hundreds of millions of lawyers sympathetic to the Labor cause.

I don't think they'd have any compunction about doing this. John Kerr was fired straight into his old job and the Liberals had to get by as best they could.

It wasn't an easy time for them but that's politics. It's dog eat what he's advised is dog out there and I don't suppose the Liberal Party would like it any more if they were in opposition and the High Court ruled on the question, for instance, of state aid for private schools.

The ruling might be the same, of course, but I don't think the Liberals would be happy to be in opposition when it happened.

Not that the Labor Party is happy in opposition, of course. They're not. They seem rather gloomy and disgruntled about it.

But they keep it to themselves in case they're accused of disrupting the system. Which seems fair, although I wouldn't mind betting they wish they'd thought of it first.

THE BROADCASTING TRIBUNAL

One of the more successful institutions in this country has been the Broadcasting Tribunal. It has enjoyed the respect of all parties and has dealt with a wide range of problems, sometimes without knowing what they were.
Media-owners got behind the Tribunal from the start.

Gidday. Now I don't know whether or not you've noticed this, but there have been some pretty curious attitudes paraded at this broadcasting inquiry I've been involved with.

And without wishing to short-circuit the present business of the Tribunal, I really do think that these people are only making trouble for themselves if they think they can alter the nature of the Australian media by pretending to establish a lot of non-monetary criteria and attempting to apply them to one of the owner-trainers. And, as I say, I mean no disrespect to the Tribunal itself, but identifying the problem in its recent history makes falling off a log look a little bit like a mensa puzzle.

For instance I was asked the other day whether or not I'd had any communication with the Minister, the Rev. Staley, before, during or after my negotiations to get control of DTV97. I hadn't been in touch with anyone from the government at all, and I said so.

But the main question surely isn't whether or not I told the government, but whether or not the government knew. If they wanted to know that, then they should have let me go, I did have a previous inquiry to go to, and they should have asked this Staley character to come in and answer a couple on his special subject.

I can see the disadvantage of this, mind you. I've seen him try to answer questions before and I'm simply not convinced that the Tribunal's got that sort of time available to it.

But more importantly, the Tribunal spent some time considering whether or not some of my newspapers had published articles that were favourably disposed to my airline. As I recall, the example given was a story in the 'Bottie' to the effect that TAA was on the brink of bankruptcy.

Of course I rejected this suggestion but only because I've trained myself to reject suggestions. My actual reaction was amazement. I presume I'm to be permitted to own everything only if I promise to pretend not to own everything, which is going to involve disabusing my employees of the impression that I employ them.

This won't bother me, but I don't know how they're going to feel about it.

A NEW HEAD

Through the work of the Broadcasting Tribunal, it became clear that changes were necessary in broadcasting. The government confronted this need, and decided that the proper place to effect changes was in the Broadcasting Tribunal.

Gidday. Now I'd like to have a word or two with you today about the Broadcasting Tribunal, because although it was an excellent idea in principle, it seems so far to have been unable to come to any clear definition of the principle under which the excellence of the idea will become clear to anyone outside the immediate family.

As you may know, the initial intention was to set up machinery whereby the general public could present its views on broadcasting and we could get some idea of what sort of improvements might be made. If any, of course. There's no judgement implied in any of this that the present system of broadcasting is anything less than totally perfect in all respects.

In order to do this, we realised we'd have to de-mystify the whole framework of broadcasting, and more particularly of course, de-legalise the forum for discussion. We didn't want the sort of set-up where we'd have a whole lot of lawyers arguing with one another in front of a benchload of other lawyers about legal niceties and matters of interpretation. We wanted the public to have free access to an independent body.

And that's what we did. We appointed a fellow to be OC the whole business and there was no question as to his independence. He used to run one of the independent channels. And although there were a few moments from time to time when it seemed as if something might work properly, it became obvious fairly early on that people were hiring lawyers to ensure that their cases were being handled properly, and pretty soon there was so much silk being waved about the place that the leader of the expedition lost track of what was going on.

So we've got a new man in to look after things, and we have no doubt about his ability to do this. He's a lawyer so he'll be very much at home with the proceedings, and he's represented a few radio stations so he's well-aware of the nature of the discussion; he doesn't watch television very much at all so he'll be fairly detached there.

So that's got the lawyers something to do. All we need now is somewhere for the public, who pay for broadcasting, and tribunals, to get together and tell someone why they think nothing works properly.

CABLE TELEVISION

New developments in broadcasting were incorporated in government policy as soon as they came to hand. In some cases, sooner.

Gidday. Now I'd like to have a word or two with you today about a remarkable technological advancement that's about to come our way. And there are several questions that need to be answered here, so we might as well get stuck straight into it. Just find yourselves a chair and make yourselves at home. Smoke if you've got them.

This shouldn't take too long. I've tried to condense everything as much as possible. But before we get on to the nuts and bolts of the thing, a few brief words about our overall approach, and I want everyone to understand this: Australia is going to have cable television.

I know it's been suggested that it might be considered perhaps slightly strange to decide to have cable television and then to have an inquiry about whether or not we're going to have it. But that's to misunderstand the purpose of the inquiry. What we're going to do is introduce cable television and then have an inquiry into whether or not we've already got it.

And I'm not anticipating a big delay here. It shouldn't take the committee too long to reach some sort of consensus in the matter, depending on who's on the committee of course. If someone comes up with a seconder for Molly Meldrum, it could run into months just explaining what a show of hands might look like.

But the main point is that after it's been decided that the minutes should be taken as read, we'll have to have a very serious look at the make-up of the industry as a whole.

Who's going to use cable television? Who's going to own it? Who's going to benefit from cable television? Who is it going to belong to? Who's going to run it? Who are the investors likely to be? Who's going to make the money out of it? How much are they going to make? Where are they going to stack it?

Then after that, of course, we can have a look at what cable television is.

A STATEMENT OF POLICY

The pace was devastating. Government policy was fraying at the edges. Definition was required. The Minister strode to the podium.

Gidday. Now a word or two further, if I may, on this business of our broadcasting policy. When I said that our policy was dynamic, I meant it was dynamic in the sense of being static, but I'd like to make the point before we go any further at all, that static is not the government's broadcasting policy.

I didn't mean that the broadcasting of static was endorsed in any way by the government; I meant, rather, that at that point the policy wasn't going anywhere. And obviously by 'anywhere' I don't mean just anywhere. I mean somewhere in particular. I mean moving directly and resolutely towards some recognisable point.

Where that point might be, of course, is dependent upon numerous other factors, which aren't very numerous and they're not factors either. What they are will depend to a great extent on the nature of technological developments as they come to hand. And we can't possibly tell what these might be because obviously they haven't happened yet.

But we have tested them. And there's no doubt in my mind that they're all going to be very suitable for our purposes. Except the ones that aren't, of course. I exclude the unsuitable ones here because I want to come back to them in a moment, and if I might just clarify something here, I think a lot of people will be quite surprised.

It's my own view, and I've been pushing this recently with some of my cabinet colleagues, that what we need in this country is a clear statement of our broadcasting requirements, and I must say I find this totally unconvincing. There must be room for the sort of diversity that inheres in such a rapidly advancing technology, and what we must remember above all, is what we did yesterday; because only by keeping a firm grip on yesterday will we be able to view tomorrow with the perspective of today.

Buy now, think later, that's our policy. And if you think it applies only to broadcasting, just leave your name when you hear the pips and we'll get someone to come round and give you a wake-up call.

TONY RESIGNS

The Minister strode away from the podium.

Gidday. Now as you'll no doubt be acutely aware by now, I've decided to get out of this business and spend a bit more time with my family. This was not suggested by the Fraser family or the Murdoch family and at no time have I been in contact with the Gyngell family.

In fact this is not a decision I've made recently at all.

I've always felt that it's a mistake to dedicate the whole of one's adult life to politics, and while not wishing to criticise the very valuable work turned in by some of the lifers up here, I have always recognised that in my own case if a job's worth doing, it's worth half-doing twice and catching the early train.

I won't deny that I found the track a bit heavy anyway, but obviously this would have been the case for anyone else in the same position.

The Broadcasting Tribunal wasn't the success it might have been, and if I had my time again, I probably wouldn't list it on the Stock Exchange. The path of the satellite didn't always run as smoothly as I'd have liked either, and with the Robinson crew so determined to own the film rights and 50 per cent of the T-shirt franchise, I was certainly pushing all manner of thing up a wide range of inclinations.

And the multi-dependant and inter-cultural broadcasting set-up was never a happy bedfellow. What went wrong here I don't know. Certainly it was my idea, but in all fairness I hadn't quite *had* the idea when I announced it, and as so often happens when an army outruns its supplies, I simply had to dig in and wait for the better weather.

97

I knew where I was of course. I'd pinpointed my position on the map and I'd put in a requisition for a paddle as long ago as April. Why it didn't arrive I'll never know, and I'm not going to guess. I've had five years of that and it's time I had a rest.

TONY BECOMES MORE RESIGNED

The Minister strode as far from the podium as he could.

Gidday. Now I'd like to have a word of two with you today about this egress I'm making from GHQ a little bit later on in our Life on Earth Year. And in particular I'd like to respond to certain allegations I couldn't help overhearing in the Despatch Department the night before last when I was over there checking that we'd managed to get my resignation sent off before the acceptance came in.

There's one thing I really would like you all to understand. Being a Member of Parliament is by no means all beer and skittles. In fact if I'd gone into the publicity side of the operation, I'd certainly have played the skittles element down to a very bare minimum indeed. It simply isn't much of a life. That's why I'm getting out. I know this might look a bit lame. I realise a lot of people think the world of politics is full of intrigue and that things are never as they seem, and I can appreciate this.

I think politics has lost a good deal of its dignity, and between ourselves that's another reason for my wanting to get out. And I'd like it known that I leave here on the very highest note in terms of my relationship with the Prime Minister.

In fact, of course, I was instrumental in some of his early attempts on the pole-vault record. We even had a double-act for a while there. I'd stand across the other side of the stage with my back against a specially designed screen, and he'd throw knives at the audience. He hit someone one year, too. The family was furious. Snedden their name was. I don't know quite what happened to them although they've stopped sending us a Xmas card and I can only assume that they never quite got over it.

Later on I supported the Prime Minister again. I blocked Supply, which accounts for the curious red swelling I sometimes get in the temples to this very day. In fact I've had a very interesting time in the last few years, and I wouldn't have missed it for the world.

And for anyone contemplating a career in politics my advice would certainly be to go ahead. Although remember to drop bread or cut blazes in trees, so you can come back out again if you get hopelessly bushed and the Sherpas all turn out to be working for someone else.

THE SATELLITE

The Minister paused briefly to discuss
another technological advancement.

Gidday. Now I've spoken about the domestic satellite
before, but I'd like to discuss it again very briefly, because it's
been decided that we're going to actually have one.

Well *we're* not, but someone's going to have one. We're not
exactly sure who, but there's been a good deal of discussion
up here about whether or not anyone's fallen for the idea that
there was any sort of discussion going on up here about who
should own it.

My view on all of this is well-known. I simply don't believe
that my family's seen enough of me. It's been a difficult
decision to make, and certain aspects of it have been of
particular concern to me.

Was there for instance some way of finding someone in an
isolated area who could get some use out of a satellite? Would
some of them prefer to have the phone on? Should the
government own a couple of screws on the upper-release-
plate section of the grommet-housing? Or should we just pay
for everything, stick it into orbit and give it away to something
beginning with P?

It was this type of question, and more especially the sort of
answer I was getting to this type of question, that put me in
mind of how pleasant it would be if I spent a little bit more
time with my family.

The satellite will be of enormous benefit to Australia, of course, because it will enable all sorts of interesting things to happen, and more importantly they'll be seen to be happening, particularly out in some of the more isolated areas. I hope there's some plan to produce a programme guide, because until they do get the phone on they won't be able to tell each other what's on. In fact, as I recall, there is a programme guide and I wouldn't mind betting the government doesn't own it either.

However, as I say, extradition proceedings are under way. Just stay there for a minute, I'll just get my hat. There's nothing much else I can do about it. In fact there hasn't been much I could do about it all along. Pass us my coat will you? Anyway good luck with it. I'm sorry we couldn't have done more for you. Perhaps if you'd got in touch with us earlier?

I've got to go now, they turn the lights out in here in a minute. I'll see you later.

THE DUST CLEARS

The decision of the Tribunal was accepted with grace and fortitude by the unfortunate billionaire.

Gidday. Now as you'll all no doubt be acutely aware by now, I've been prevented from owning the television station I own, by the as-yet-unexplained whim of the broadcasting troika.

Before I take any questions from the floor, let me disavow you completely of the view that this is a systems entry and we're all just changing hats until after the democracy on the 18th. Certainly we'll be appealing against the decision, and certainly this will take time, and certainly the appeal won't be heard until well after the democracy, but it's nevertheless a pretty serious business and we're not taking it lightly at all.

Unfortunately, both the people with whom we had no communication whatsoever during the various stages of the takeover have taken their bat and ball and headed for lower ground. Which is one of the problems, of course, because as we've been saying for some time now, the place is groaning with precedent, for breaking the law with the intention of sending a few of the lads from maintenance out later on to clean up the mess and repair the fencing, and I don't really see why our particular enterprise has been singled out and made an example of.

Aside from anything else it's been an extremely costly business, and for me to divest myself of equity in the company would be a very difficult exercise indeed.

The resolution of this whole sorry affair is obviously going to depend to some extent on whether or not we can find a minister somewhere who's prepared to spend a bit less time with his family and a bit more time with mine.

The whole point of the takeover in the first place was to get a better deal for the Australian public, and as a part-time member of this body I must say I've seldom seen a better deal.

The appeal has yet to be mounted at this stage of course, and, as I say, it will take time, and of course time is money, I'm delighted to say.

A FLAT TAX RATE

Any suggestion that the Treasury has
made a decision, particularly one
suggested by the Country Party, must be
looked at very closely indeed.

Gidday. Now I'd like to have a word or two with you today about the flat tax rate we're not thinking of introducing at all. This is a point I've made before. I've always had doubts about the social justice of the idea and I don't really think such a system is a realistic alternative.

But I do want to mention it again and outline my reservations for you, because I understand certain of my sparring partners are thinking of trying to pass it off as a patent medicine up in the Queensland area. We're having a couple of by-elections in the region and somebody blew the dust off the idea the other night while campaigning for the vote of the over-privileged.

I must say I don't regard it as a very responsible ploy, and I'm bound to say I don't think it's a very good tax. One of the examples given was that there would be something like a 20 per cent tax rate on all income. I'm not sure how like 20 per cent it would be. I wouldn't think it would be very like 20 per cent. In fact I'd be surprised if it didn't end up having a more than passing resemblance to 40 per cent, but that's academic at this stage anyway.

It was then suggested that in order to protect the less well-off, there'd have to be a level established and no income below it would be taxed at all. I don't know where they're going to put the big blue pencil-mark but if it's anywhere north of about $1.50, the Treasury will be taking in washing by April.

Doug Anthony said at one stage that one of the more lustrous benefits of the scheme was that it would help stamp out tax avoidance. I imagine that the basis for this claim was that it would stamp out the *need* for tax avoidance, although I'm not convinced that if the people at work in the tax-avoidance industry were suddenly bundled across into the unemployed department, there'd be more than a couple of dozen people holding down any real sort of yacker anywhere on the island.

The main thing is that we don't let our differences get out of hand here. After all, we're two parties united under one pair of banners, and although we're a coalition, we've ultimately got only one leader and that, of course, is each.

THE COST OF
THE HIGH COURT

As the building of the High Court in Canberra neared completion, suggestions began to appear in the press concerning the possibility that the cost was perhaps slightly extraordinary. This feeling spread to a more general disrespect for management. So much so that comment became necessary.

Gidday. Now I don't normally get hysterical, and I think to break entirely with tradition at this stage would probably be seen as a less than rational response.

But on the other hand the fact that a campaign of villification is being mounted against my person is something of a worry to me, and I don't say this solely in response to what's been said so far, which after all hasn't been extensive or indeed very frightening. But as the election moves relentlessly towards our present position, I can see now that disclosures and vituperative hoo-ha will be paraded in the press and I want to pre-empt as much of it as I possibly can.

Firstly, let me respond immediately to the suggestion that things have got perhaps slightly out of hand with the building of the High Court. This is out of order but I'll answer it anyway.

I defy anyone to build a $50 million building for an amount of money less than it costs. It simply can't be done.

Of course the exercise has been pretty severely trimmed since we began. Initially the building was to be slightly more substantial, in fact with a door in each state and with a rather charming little baroque railway system fashioned of gold and with comfortable seating made of larks uvulas.

This whole concept has been completely axed now. The modesty of the present construction is almost pathetic, so there's really no mileage in sounding off about the wasting of millions of dollars on an extravagant monument to nothing at all.

And to insinuate that the project was somehow handed to me, in some darkly conceived consideration for my having given an opinion in the matter of Kerr v. All That's Pure and Decent, is utterly without any shred of reality.

And let me, while I've got the floor, which incidentally is no longer being made of moonrock (this is a standard wooden floor with only a very light polish and some inlaid French miniatures in the knot-holes), let me say that when I said I'd never heard of a company which later turned out to own my house and of which I appear to be something of a director, and which hasn't lodged an annual return since the Plaintiff came to power in 1975, I didn't mean I hadn't heard of it, I meant I hadn't heard the question.

However I've got a feeling it'll probably be asked again.

THE FAMILY COMPANY

Rather than being put asunder, the
rumours gathered momentum.

Gidday. Now I suspected that this might happen. In fact I said just the other day that this might happen. The Labor Party's campaign against my person has been formally announced in the House and of course the press, bereft as it is of anything worthwhile to address itself to, has picked the story up and has been trying to squeeze a bit of cheap mileage out of it, which I must say doesn't surprise me at all.

However, just to set the record straight on a couple of points, and I haven't got long, we're putting up the curtains in the Hyperbole this afternoon and they cost a million dollars a metre without the lining, so I want to get down there as soon as possible just to make sure things are going to plan.

But as I say, a couple of points before I rush off.

Firstly, I was most disturbed by the reaction to my statement that the company which owns my house, a company with which incidentally I personally have no connection whatsoever, is a family company.

This seems a simple and unequivocal enough statement but no sooner had it been made than someone from the parliament, and I don't have to go into much detail about what I think of the parliament, got up and said how could it be a purely family concern when the most substantial shareholder is L. J. Thompson who has no connection with the family?

How anyone can say this sort of thing I'll never understand.

How can anyone claim that a man has no connection with the family when he runs the family company? How he's supposed to run the family company without having at least some sort of very occasional peripheral connection with the family, I don't know.

Aside from anything else, as I said in the first place, the person who has no connection with my family company is myself. Other people are obviously connected with it. Someone's got to be or it wouldn't work properly.

And quite clearly the people who run it are in touch with the family. If they weren't, I couldn't possibly know what was going on.

And if I didn't know what was going on with my own family company, no sane man would give me $50 million to fiddle about building a Hyperbole.

MORE TROUBLE

Unfavourable opinion persisted.

Gidday. Now as you will understand, I'm a very busy man. We're having a team of farriers in this afternoon to nail the gold-leaf on to the insides of the light sockets down at the Hyperbole, so as you can appreciate I haven't got a lot of time to spend on this, but perhaps I might clear the air even further by making just one or two points I think could profitably be considered.

I read somewhere recently that there was some question that because my family company, with which I have no connection at all, was a shareholder in certain other companies, with which I therefore have no connection at all, there might be a possibility that my opinion in cases involving these companies might perhaps be slightly less objective than if it weren't; and it wasn't; and I can tell you now that it isn't.

This is like saying that because I'm a taxpayer, I'm going to take the side of the government in all cases where the other litigant is a private company other than one with which I have a vicarious lack of connection through the family concern.

Or that because I'm a member of the human race I'm likely to come out in favour of other humans if ever they come before the bench, which is obviously absurd, because they never do.

The Prime Minister has quite rightly defended me, and I don't want a lot of childish suggestion that I'll somehow contrive to favour his position in legal matters.

111

In fact to my knowledge he's only ever asked me for an opinion on one occasion and, as I recall, it didn't even come to court. I can't even remember what it was now.

The most important thing is that we get the Hyperbole finished before some clown in the accounts department decides to lower the boom.

Already there's some talk that the internal moat we're filling with ass's milk so that the judges can whistle about the building in barges, be cut back to a single lane, which in my view will cause more problems than it solves.

A SLIGHT COMPLICATION

Ultimately the building was finished.
So too, the biography.

Gidday. Well as you're all no doubt acutely aware, the Hyperbole went under the hammer last week and was knocked down to the Australian public for an undisclosed figure believed to be in the region of $50 million plus costs. And I can understand their excitement at having secured the property and having thereby at least nominally prevented it from falling to overseas ownership.

I know there's been a lot of talk about the cost of building the thing in the first place, but I'm sure that now, as the spotlight of publicity swings away and we're left with the business of getting on with the day-to-day affairs of the law itself, the ferocity of the discussion will wane slightly and in a couple of years people will start forgetting the details and when we stick them in the box they'll go to pieces entirely, and we'll trip them up on dates and hair colours and things, and none of it'll stick.

This has certainly been the case with the other jobs I've worked on and if the worst comes to the worst, I understand we don't have an extradition arrangement with certain parts of Surrey.

However, this is not what I want to talk about. I understand that there's been a book published about me. Now I didn't authorise this book and I must say I find myself in some confusion as to precisely what action to take.

The idea that something can happen in this country without my authorisation is abhorrent to me, as it obviously is to many of you. It flies directly in the face of everything this country has come to stand for, and this country has been bent over backwards in an effort to make it stand for just about anything.

On the other hand of course, one can do little but fall to the ground in admiration of the subject of the tome. And I must say I was delighted to be praised at the launching for having remained in Australia after 1975. I was a bit worried for a while that this might look like effrontery but if I'm going to be lionised, I suppose I'll have to find in favour of Mr Iscariot provided he's got the gall to stay here.

A GRACEFUL DEPARTURE

Eventually, retirement comes to us all;
sometimes early, sometimes
almost unbelievably late.

Gidday. Now I'd like to have a word or two with you today about the assessments I've seen here and there in the past couple of weeks of my lengthy career in the various echelons of the law in this country.

Most people have pointed out that I was a brilliant advocate. Some have even suggested that I was the most brilliant advocate of my day. Although why the slight qualification there I don't know.

But I'd like to address particularly the needless insinuation that it was the power and range of my almost unbelievable skill at advocacy that somehow prejudiced my performance when I assumed the position of ultimate guardian of truth and building-projects.

This is quite simply not the case. It's not supported by any of the rather loose and tawdry factual evidence we've seen paraded before us, and any attempt to draw a proper conclusion from such hearsay is destined not to succeed.

The suggestion seems to be, insofar as it seems to be anything, that my advocacy was at its most impressive when I was advocating my own opinion.

This doesn't bear a lot of analysis and it represents a comprehensive failure to read the constitution correctly. But let's look at it briefly by all means.

In recent years my opinion has been interpretative of the law itself, and by and large the proper interpretation of the law is that above and beyond anything else, present company excepted of course, the law is the law. There are times when there needs to be some definition of what the law means, but ultimately its main function, beyond even meaning something, is that it be the law. And when this has been forgotten, as it has been from time to time, there's certainly a need for someone to point it out.

There may be something in the pointing out of it, that calls for some measure of advocacy, but advocacy is by no means the principal element in it, and advocacy of one's own opinion has nothing whatever to do with it.

I have had opinions on some of these matters of course. It would be unfair on the surgeon for me to pretend otherwise, but in the final analysis the law is unimpeachably the law, except on the odd occasion when it is unimpeachably what it is said to be.

PEACEFUL PURPOSES

UN to Study Pretoria 'Bomb Test'

Age, 29 October 1979

Gidday. Now I couldn't help noticing the other day that someone has exploded a nuclear device somewhere in an area best described as the lower portion of that part of the world generally regarded as being perhaps slightly more African than some of the other regions.

Let me say immediately that I'm not suggesting that any-body in particular exploded a bomb. In fact we're not even sure it was a bomb, it could have been something else, perhaps an antelope or something. It could have been just a nuclear explosion purely and simply with no cause whatsoever and nothing to do with any human beings at all. Although I should point out that while this theory is not without its attractions, it is regarded by the bulk of scientific opinion as bordering on the very unlikely indeed, and it is widely recognised that someone did actually explode a nuclear bomb.

I know it's hard to accept this. I've been grappling with it for nearly a week now myself, and I can still only barely conceal my surprise. The real question is whose bomb was it?

Let me say right away that it had nothing whatsoever to do with South Africa. The South African authorities have made this quite clear, and I must say that the suggestion that it might have been South Africa who exploded a nuclear bomb in the sea off the coast of South Africa struck me as being fairly ridiculous when I first heard it. In order to explode a nuclear bomb, a country would have to have rather a lot of enemies, which South Africa hasn't got at all, so there's no need for a bomb; and they'd have to be enormously wealthy because nuclear bombs tend to run into money, and South Africa is among the poorest nations on earth, so they couldn't possibly afford one.

It's been suggested that the Russians lost a missile some-where near South Africa in 1963, and that it's only just exploded. This is impossible, because there's no such thing as a nuclear accident. And it couldn't have been an American bomb, because the President hasn't formally denied that it is. And it can't be that we've been given bodgie information, because if nuclear accidents are impossible, the instruments designed to record them would be infallible.

I thought for a while it might have been Lord Lucan, but there's no report that the explosion had a moustache. I don't know. It wouldn't worry me normally, but I think that if we're going to sell uranium to people, we have a right to know who it is we're selling it to, and why they won't own up when one of their peaceful purposes goes off by mistake.

UPGRADING DEFENCE

Defence is obviously a constant
priority for the Australian Government,
who think they're being followed.

Gidday. Now it looks already as if my remarks about national defence have been completely misunderstood, and I must say in all honesty I half-expected this to happen.

There seems to be practically no one out there with the faintest knowledge of military strategy, and I think the public at large is going to have very little appreciation of the peril in which this country stands, until the streets of Perth are ringing with the hoof beats of the Czar's cavalry.

Even the simplest exposition of our defence policy seems to go over the heads of most Australians, and it's with this fundamental national inadequacy in mind that I'm now going to explain the elements of our defence. And I'm only going to do it once, so get it into you.

First of all, in order to defend ourselves, it's not necessary that we be attacked. We can think we're being attacked, or we can imagine ourselves being attacked, or we can conceive of circumstances in which we'd be fairly certain to be attacked. So, rather than actually fighting, defence has become to a great extent the business of preparedness, and I think the Baden-Powell family would be justifiably proud of the policy being implemented by your government.

Of course defences have to be renewed and re-assessed all the time to keep pace with technological advancements and the eddy and flow of political fortunes throughout the known world. And at the moment the Australian defensive network is on a par with the very most sophisticated available in any country, in about the 12th century. So we're going to update it. We're going to get some F111's in.

I don't think anyone would deny that the F111 is one of the most dangerous aircraft that ever put to sea. We're going to get the Americans to visit our ports more often and there's even been mention of bringing the HMAS *Melbourne* into the fray, which is a pretty serious threat to anything that floats. By about August we'll be keeping pace with the 16th century and ready to make an all-out assault on the election.

Unfortunately this will mean the tax cuts might have to leave just after the interval to catch the 4.35 but if you look at the small print, you'll see that it was subject to change without notice by management, and between ourselves it wasn't really a tax cut anyway.

But I'll tell you about that another day when I've got less time.

DEFENCE DEVELOPMENT IN THE AIR

The government has kept the public informed at every stage, largely out of a sense of courtesy.

Gidday. Now I don't want to worry you, but I really don't see how I can keep this from you. What I would like though is some sort of assurance that you won't panic and behave in an unseemly manner when you hear it.

You might notice in the course of the next few months, in fact you might have noticed it already; I don't know exactly when the balloon's supposed to go up officially on this business, but there will probably be at some relatively early juncture large black shapes moving across the skies above the city. I'm not sure whether there'll be groups of large shapes all moving along in skeins, or whether there'll be just the odd individual shape blocking out the sun for only a very short period. But there will be shapes, and I don't want you to worry about them. They're friendly shapes.

In an attempt to frighten the Russians completely out of their jodhpurs, we've arranged for Australia to become a sort of playground for the American air force.

I just forget precisely how this is supposed to frighten the Russians, but the way it was put to me in the extensive and wide-ranging discussions I had for about a quarter of an hour in Washington the other day, it seemed like a pretty strong measure. It petrified me when I first heard it and I can only assume that the Russians, whose paranoia is well-known, will find the whole thing a fairly chastening experience.

Now the planes will tend, of course, in the terms of the agreement, to be bombers, and if anything falls out of them, I must ask you not to touch it. Just leave it alone, and move as discreetly as you can, in the direction of away.

If you see a big kind of door arrangement underneath the aircraft swing open suddenly and release a lot of rather solid looking things that you think might be bombs, just give us a call and we'll make appropriate representation through official channels, and we'll see if we can't get some sort of undertaking from allied GHQ that everything's OK, or that perhaps if it isn't, they'll come to the party to some extent in the clean-up operation.

I'll get out of your way now, and you will too if you've got any brains.

PEACEFUL PURPOSES WITH HINDSIGHT

Unfortunately the bomb that wasn't
exploded near South Africa, was spotted
by a satellite, and questions were asked.
Silly, silly questions.

Gidday. Now I feel I should have a word or two with you about the very substantial bomb that wasn't exploded anywhere near South Africa around about Grand Final time.

I've spoken about this before and I had hoped that the matter was settled, but I see from the tissues that in sharp contrast with settling, the matter hasn't even been found yet. And I think this is part of the problem.

There's been something observed by a special satellite whose job it is to go off-course every now and then, and observe things without knowing what they are, and there are several theories about precisely what it was that didn't happen. I don't want to worry you, but if you've got anyone there who subscribes to the 'Peaceful Purposes Monthly', it might be an idea to just get them to run down to the shops for a couple of minutes while we discuss the mouse trap.

The first alternative is that the South Africans, whose support for the notion of black nationalism is conditional upon clause 1 of the legislation involving the freezing over of Hell, have exploded a neutron bomb which has solved the problem of radio-active fallout, and hasn't been noticed by the most advanced bangmeters and wallop-gauges known to man. It's so technologically superior to tired old rubbish like

A-bombs and H-bombs and more particularly, of course, swords and machines that throw rocks at buttresses, that it hasn't even been detected by satellites. And all the seismological boffins can say about it is the date, which was probably in most of the papers and isn't going to be of any major assistance if one of these curious machines makes some sort of egress from an aircraft anywhere near anything at all.

There's another theory that the great white hopelessness is part-owned by the Israelis, and there's even a suggestion that the French might have one, which would account for the fact that rather a lot of tropical fish were a bit off-colour in about 1978.

But the ownership of the hardware is a secondary consideration anyway. It merely helps to define the nationalities of the people who pick up the silver medal in WW3.

In fact it might not be a bad idea if we earmark a spot somewhere in the fertile crescent, and put up a sombre but tasteful little memorial to indicate the grave of the unknown race.

Of course it might all be a mistake. I'll ask around and get back to you.

THE REPORT ON SECURITY

Australian national security suffered a slight setback when the report on Australia's national security went what could only be described as missing.

Gidday. Now I was going to have a few words with you today about national security.

I think it's important for us to have some knowledge of how a security system operates, particularly during a period when international links are undergoing certain stresses, and of course the internal network is reflecting the pressures of constant re-assessment and high re-definition.

But unfortunately the report seems to have been mislaid.

We're not exactly sure at this stage quite what's happened to it, but we've had a bloke in with a fine tooth-comb and he's been having a pretty comprehensive rummage for the best part of the last week, which was Saturday afternoon, and he hasn't been able to locate the actual report at all.

Either that, or he's found it but then lost it again, and he didn't like to mention the fact that for a while it was found.

Anyway, that's not important. We've had a report done on the first report and, of course, particularly on how it was that a report on Australia's internal security should behave in such a paradoxical fashion.

The second report I myself haven't seen, but I know someone who's met a person who thinks he might have seen it on a train in Adelaide the day before yesterday. Admittedly, he only saw it from behind, but he reckons he'd know it anywhere and there seems very little doubt that if it wasn't the second report, then it was something very like it, possibly even the first report, or perhaps the third.

We did have a third report done, but it slipped away at the unveiling and hasn't been seen since.

The report on how that happened, I have seen. A bloke in an overcoat showed me the first few pages of it in the upstairs bar of a pub that I notice isn't there anymore.

We are having a fifth report done, and the people who are doing it are bolted to the floor in my office.

It's not going to be easy for them, and I must ask you all in the meantime to report anything suspicious you might see being duplicated and sent all over the world. And if you've helped any government departments across the street recently, I must ask you to get in touch with someone about it, if you can find anyone.

I'm not sure what's going on anymore myself. No one's answering the phone at the front gate and if someone doesn't slide some sandwiches under my door by nightfall, I'll get on to the ONA and speak to Mr Orwell myself, personally.

NUCLEAR WASTES

Science is frequently accused of lacking responsibility in not thinking about side effects. This criticism is grossly unfair.

Gidday. Now I was delighted to see that it's been suggested in America that nuclear wastes be packed into rockets and put into orbit around the Sun. And I pride myself that I know a good idea when I see one, even if the light's going.

But there is one aspect of the proposal that does bother me slightly, and I don't want to worry you, but I feel you ought to know in plenty of time in case you want to leave a forwarding address.

It does look at this stage, and it's early nights yet admittedly, but there does seem to be an outside possibility that a contingency plan will need to be mapped out in case there's some sort of technical hitch during the period known, for filing purposes, as lift-off. And I'm ignoring here the likelihood that the solar postal authorities might return the odd consignment to sender, due to inadequate packaging.

But as I say, the main worry with this otherwise extremely responsible idea, is that if a rocket-load of dangerous nuclear wastes comes into some sort of conflict with general Newtonian precepts before getting out past the things that hold up the Van Allen trousers, it will be drawn inexorably back towards the world as we know it.

In my view this will happen in one of two places. Either it'll come straight back down on to the blocks, if it hasn't got very far before the impossible happens, or if there's a problem after lift-off itself, the thing might come to rest somewhere else.

If they manage to prevent it from paying a full state visit to another country, it might land in the sea, which will obviously present another problem. They'll have to devise a method of getting something from the bottom of the ocean up into orbit around the Sun, and of course anything that's been contaminated will have to be given the elbow as well.

Although how they're going to put the sea into orbit around the Sun I don't know.

HOSTAGE CRISIS

The attempted raid on Iran to liberate the American hostages was explained in detail. There was nevertheless some doubt about the planning.

Gidday. Now I'd like to have a word or two with you about a matter of the very gravest consequence, and I'm not fooling about here. I want to get this business out in the open, take a couple of general questions from the floor, and get out before the feeling goes in my legs.

I understand that there's been some suggestion in America that the full story has yet to be told about the abortive raid conducted in Iran. I gather that some moron is claiming that had we got into the area where the hostages were, we had no adequate means of getting them out; and that the story about having to pull out because the air filter fell off one of the helicopters is perhaps not as convincing as it might be.

I don't know who this maniac is, and I don't much care either, really. There's always a fringe element prepared to completely abandon reason for the sake of hectoring decent society. According to this loon, we were going into Iran to shoot the hostages, get out again, blame the Iranians; and go back in again with a punitive force amounting to the biggest surprise anyone's ever seen. And the reason we didn't do it, according to this theory, was that President Carter somehow found out about it and blew the whistle.

I don't really want to grace this obvious gobbledegook with any real degree of plausibility by responding to it in too much detail, but I think there are a couple of points I might make.

Firstly, it hasn't been made clear how we were going to get the hostages out. But now the security blanket has been lifted, I can reveal to you that we were going to get the first two or three out in a brown paper bag to go for help, and the rest we were going to give an all-day travel-anywhere bus voucher, and then meet them back at the corral.

Incidentally now the security has been cleared, I can reveal that we were only in Chile to pick up some dry-cleaning, and otherwise we haven't been out of the house for years.

COMPUTER WAR

The American defence network was alerted
when the computerised warning system
indicated that the Russians were coming.

Gidday. Now there is a question, of course, that presents
itself as a result of the fact that the nuclear war was averted
the other day only when it was discovered that it hadn't
happened. And it's a luxury to be able to even consider this
point.

I myself am very grateful for the opportunity. I'm humbled to realise just how insignificant man is, and how little power he really has in the world when compared with the serene beauty of gnat-birth.

However, life goes on, until further notice, and I must say I was comforted to see Australia's strategic capability so rapidly increased. Given that Russia's role in the recent very close shave was not to have attacked America, it's quite clear that any other nation embarking on such a reckless course of action can reasonably expect to be obliterated, unless someone spots a stray bleep somewhere and reins the system in before we go into injury time.

On this basis every country on earth is a contender, although I would imagine that our favoured-nation status would ensure that the Americans would let us know if we ever launched a lack-of-attack against them. I think it would be only fair, in the light of our long-standing servitude, that we be given a couple of minutes to throw on a sunhat before the temperature changes.

I'm personally very gratified that warfare has at last become a bit refined. Gone are the days when people came down like wolves on folds, and one was actually confronted by an enemy. Now not only has the physical presence of the enemy been eliminated, and his intention pre-empted, but the perception of these fundamentally unsound military abstracts has been entrusted to a machine which can apparently conceive of things independently of their existence.

This is a relief to me. I've said for a long time, certainly since Yalta, that the best form of defence is a computer with a dodgy grommet-housing. The only important thing yet to be decided is whether or not computers are only as good as the information fed into them by people, and whether or not the reverse is also true.

A SHAMEFUL POSITION

Laos, Vietnam and North Korea announced that they would participate in the Moscow Olympics. This worried the Prime Minister.

Gidday. Now I'd like to have a word or two with you today about the very disparate views that now exist in this society with regard to the Eisteddfod.

This has nothing at all to do with the imposition of trade sanctions on Hungary, and I mention this only because we seem to have imposed trade sanctions on Hungary. And Rumania. We've imposed trade sanctions on Rumania too. These countries are both potentially big markets for Australia, but they haven't been spending as freely as we'd like, so it was thought we should perhaps give the trade a bit of a jiggle-along.

And if the Russian experience is anything to go by, while most of the punters are out the front trying to get the Embargo to stand upright on its pedestal, you and a few other moral imperatives can be out the back ladelling rubles in through the spare-bedroom window with a front-end loader, and a heyho for Anthony Rowley.

But that's not what I want to talk about. I want to clarify something I said recently about the shameful position I find myself in.

This, as you may know, was a reference to our being bracketed in the second division with Laos, Vietnam and North Korea.

This has been misunderstood. Obviously I've got no intention of being gratuitously nasty about these places. I've visited them all at various stages. Korea I knew when it belonged to the Huntingdon family. And Pol Pot certainly isn't officer material.

I'm not denying that most of the democracies of Western Europe are going to the Eisteddfod, or that some countries are being paid not to go, or that roughly the same number of countries are going to Moscow as went to Montreal. What I would say is that circumstances change all the time, and so should we. Well, the Federation should, anyway.

I'm all right, I've been in a shameful position from the beginning.

THE DEFENCE ALLIANCE

Australia's alliance with America was less
complicated than many people thought.

Gidday. Now I'd like to have a word or two with you about this country's defence. This is important and it's bound to come up sooner or later, so I would ask that you pay proper attention so you know which muster station you're supposed to go to.

You may have seen some mention in the trade press of B52's and various other items of American haberdashery we've arranged to provide billeting facilities for. Obviously there's some reciprocity in these arrangements. The Americans are providing the aircraft, and we're providing landing space, in this case Australia.

And it should be quite clearly understood that this is all part of a defence policy based on mutual aid, and I'll tell you how this works. If Australia is attacked by someone from around here somewhere, and the fight doesn't actually affect America directly, then they can choose whether or not they'd like to become involved. They might decide to come in with us; they might have other things to do.

Similarly of course, if America becomes involved in some sort of conflict with something beginning with R, and we decide that it's got nothing to do with us and we'd rather just sit on about eighteen, then we won't be obliged to have anything whatever to do with it.

Except for the fact that America has bases here and if the hegemonous lawyers are really on their toes, they might put someone in the box and ask for a definition of neutrality.

What this means in general terms is that if you hear a loud bang, and more particularly of course if you see a loud bang, try not to get too carried away about it. It might not have anything to do with us.

Although if it's really loud and you can't sleep or something, by all means write to us here at the department.

MISSING DOCUMENTS

There was consternation when it was discovered that a New South Wales Labor Party branch office had been broken into, and documents stolen. It was difficult to understand why this outrage had occurred.

Gidday. Now I'm given to understand by our archivist up here, Storeman Drang, that certain documents of an extremely sensitive nature have gone missing, and in order to clear the air I've consented to make a few remarks along the following lines.

Firstly, of course, it hardly needs saying that it's a regrettable thing to have happened, and we all hope the criminals are apprehended in due course and brought to justice.

In fact I can do better than that, I can give you the name of the Justice we'd like them brought to. No? No, I can see heads wagging, and I sense that to do that at this time would be inappropriate.

It saddens me though, that our society has reached a point where even the private records of an organisation such as this can be plundered with such apparent ease. Of course it's happened to others, a couple of councils, various business houses; even the budget was talked out of its homing instincts.

The stuff that went missing from here wasn't very important, and I don't even know why anyone would want it.

It was just a little wad of nonsense about some investments we made a few years ago with the Sleight of Hand Bank. This was in the days when the Bank was OK, of course, and they paid us back at whatever rate was agreed to.

I just forget what the rate was now. Something fairly standard. If I had the accountant's rough working sheets, I could tell you exactly what it was.

But unfortunately, that information seems to have been what the spring cleaning was all about. You can take it from me though, that there was nothing dodgy about the interest rate. There's no suggestion that the interest rate was particularly high, or that it was waived altogether, or that there were two interest rates, one from the Bank to me and another from me to the consolidated account.

I can't really see why anyone would want to remove this information at all, and there were a couple of phone numbers on the back of it I wouldn't mind either.

THE ALICE SPRINGS TO DARWIN RAILWAY

When a government announces changes in its defence policy, it is sometimes necessary to explain the military value of certain aspects of it. There is normally a simple explanation.

Gidday. Now I'd like to explain to you if I may, the role to be played in the defence of this country by the Alice Springs-to-Darwin railway line.

And I must say, certain of the strategic advantages seem pretty obvious to me. There is, for instance, the facility for shifting things from Alice Springs to Darwin if we're attacked from the north, or from Darwin to Alice Springs, of course, if we're attacked from the centre. Or from Alice Springs to Darwin and back again if we're attacked from the north and we want to keep out of the way for a while, but we left something in Darwin before the balloon went up.

But above and beyond that, we'll be able to move stuff about up there with a pretty free hand. Train travel is very rapid. Of course we haven't actually timed a nuclear warhead in flight between Darwin and Alice Springs, but there doesn't seem any real doubt that the smart money would be on the train. Anything marked urgent would probably have to be on the interballistic missile, of course, but there'd have to be something on the train or there wouldn't be any point in running the thing.

The other advantage in having a railway line in a time of war is that it's practically impossible to destroy. It's just about dead straight for a start, so you've got to be pretty accurate to bomb it. If anyone did bomb it, all we'd have to do would be send out a group of our engineering people from one of the many bases we'll be setting up every two or three hundred thousand miles along the vital artery.

It's hardly likely to be bombed really, because of the great possibilities out there for camouflage. I don't know whether you've ever flown over the area, but it's certainly not going to be a complete pushover spotting a railway line strung out across the extremely hilly and bushy terrain. There's not much actual bush up there at the moment. They've been having a bit of a dry patch up there for a while, but we'll run some bush up there as soon as we get the line built.

Now someone will pass among you with a hat, just drop your vote in, We'll be around for the money later.

ASIO vs
THE HIGH COURT

The role of Australia's secret service is
defined from time to time, so that the
citizens are kept informed about the
enormous power they have.

Gidday. Now I don't know whether or not you noticed
this, but it has now been decided officially that ASIO is above
the law, and I must say it's comforting to see a behavioural
tendency at last fortified by the weight of judicial opinion.

And there's no question about the finality of this decision,
because it was made by the High Court, and the High Court
is not responsible to anyone either. This doesn't mean that
these bodies are not responsible, it simply means that if they
are, they can't tell anyone.

The only major decision to be made at this stage is whether it's the High Court or ASIO who's the market leader.

The High Court would have to be the pre-race favourite. Not only is it not responsible to anyone, ultimately of course it is the law, so to some extent it's above itself. Which is a feat very seldom performed outside the Chipp family, and certainly not a thing often seen in the public life, which is another thing we won't be seeing a lot of.

But my money is on ASIO. Not only are they above the law which is above itself, but the air's so rarified up there that no one even knows who they are. There's no real question about what they do of course. We're probably all fairly clear about that. They find things out. They find things out about all sorts of things. In fact, I don't think I'd be betraying too important a confidence if I divulged to you that on a really good day, they can find things out about various different aspects of all sorts of things.

I'm sorry I can't be more specific than this. I'd like to be able to be, but it is an Australian organisation, and I'm no good to you. I live in Australia.

DIFFERENCES IN DEFENCE POLICIES

When there are substantial differences
in the defence policies of the major parties,
it is important that the public is made
aware. Even if only slightly.

Gidday. Now I'd like to have a word or two with you about defence, and I mention this only because it looks at the moment as if the Yippee-Yi-Yo Party might get in in America. And if Ronnie ever had any credibility at all in the foreign affairs area, there seems very little doubt that it was completely defenestrated with the news that one of his advisers will be the thoroughly dependable R. M. Nixon, whose attitude to foreign policy seems to have been very closely linked to the concept of Bang.

The two major electoral platforms in Australia differ slightly on how they're going to ignore this.

Malcolm plans to ignore it altogether, and worry about the Russians, who represent a much more serious threat because we don't know a lot about them. We know a bit about their wheat requirements and how much wool they think they can handle, but we know very little about them personally, and consequently we're considerably imperilled by them.

But the attitude of the Labor Party will really take you to the fair. They plan to let the Americans fly in and out of the place, but only if there are no nuclear weapons involved.

As far as I can see there are three main ways of finding this out. Firstly, of course, we could ask them. This might not work, but it would be a very great honour, and I don't think we should dismiss it altogether.

Secondly, we could spy on them, which I think we can dismiss altogether, and thirdly and perhaps more realistically, we could guess. This would have the added advantage of being consistent not only with the rest of our defence policy, but with our policies on everything else as well.

I suggest that if the American election is won by Ronald, we have a very serious think about how far we're prepared to go with the alliance. We'll have to have a meeting about it of course, although for the sake of safety I suggest we don't have it in the world.

Let's just go somewhere quiet, and see if we can't steam our signatures off a few things.

THE SECURITY NETWORK

Australia's security network is often subjected to a lot of ignorant and destructive criticism. If permitted to develop unchecked, this might harm the effectiveness of a very clever system.

Gidday. Now about the business of Australia's security, or the security of Australia's business as we like to call it down at the Bureau, and the Bureau *is* a front. Before people start writing in about what they see as a massive deception, let me make one or two points that apparently haven't occurred to anyone.

Firstly, you'll find if you go right back through your records and recall any conversations you've had, either with the people in the front office, or the rather more shadowy personnel who get into the building from the back lane adjacent to the glue factory on the northern side of our despatch bay, you'll find for yourselves that no one has ever denied that among our various and divers other functions, is that of being guardian of this country's security interests.

In fact, people have commented quite frequently on the very large number of furtive-looking persons who have tended to come and go quite freely from the various offices and agencies of the company. I'm not going to run away from this. It's not something I've ever been ashamed of, and neither do I see it as a very remarkable admission.

Obviously we're not the only group to be involved. There are others. That's what a network is.

But above and beyond my own connection with Australian secret intelligence, and nowhere is the secret of intelligence better kept than in this country, I would like to say something about the suggestion that the Americans are running a much more sophisticated operation here than anyone's prepared to admit, and that we don't really know what day it is.

Let me say that whenever the national security is threatened, we're there.

The Nugan Hand Bank was a good example of this. Here was an international business house where one of the principals threw a pretty bad sickie and the other one's tying up some loose ends, and seems to have gone perhaps to Queensland droving, and I'm not suggesting that anyone had anything to do with the CIA. At all. I saw somewhere that the CIA used it to shift money through Asia into Europe, but I didn't believe it. Didn't believe it for a moment.

But if anything a little bit dodgy did go on, and the national security was even slightly at risk, you can bet your boots that our intelligence people will find out about it. As soon as it hits the papers, the information will be analysed, photographed, and left in suitcases behind trees.

CHANGES AT HEAD OFFICE

Reagan's Walkover

Financial Review, 6 November 1980

Gidday. Now I'd like to have a word or two with you today about some of the more memorable aspects of recent events up in the Washington office. And of course our defence policy is now largely determined by Central Casting, so it's of more than passing interest to us that the lead role in the next few episodes of the American dream has now officially been secured by Trigger.

He was signed up the other day, at a simple little ceremony consistent with the traditional American reserve, and notable principally for the phrase 'to the best of my ability'.

I don't want to cavil about this, I've got a fair bit of other cavilling work on at the moment, but this does look like a get-out clause to me.

On the other hand, of course, I do recognise that the appointment of Pavlov's Dog as the Secretary of State will probably see the get-out clause fall into pretty severe disuse as a concept on a more or less global basis.

A lot of people are obviously concerned about the Great Ronaldo, but in his defence, let me point out that he's a man of great experience. He was Governor of California for a while and I remember being right behind him when he was the Deputy Mayor of Cheyenne for an hour and a half in about 1954.

But he has the added advantage of being the 40th President, and being the only one in history to have known all the others personally.

So, the scope of his knowledge is considerable, and aside from anything else, if he forgets his lines and wipes a few principalities off the map up near the Fertile Crescent, we can always edit the end of the world out, and re-shoot the last bit with the emphasis on something you wouldn't mind taking the kids to.

HUMAN RIGHTS
POLICY DROPPED

It is important that a new government put
its stamp on the administration of the
nation. And on anything else it doesn't
like the look of.

*NB: STERILISED
CATTLE PROD

Gidday. Now I suppose many of you sensed, as we did
here, a wave of very genuine relief at the recent announcement from the head office in Washington that the human
rights policy, so often alluded to by the previous area sales
manager, has been fed into the shredder, and is no more. I
realise that this pre-supposes that Jimmy had a human rights
policy, but by comparison with the intended lack-of-human-
rights policy, any country with a pedestrian crossing is a
hotbed of airfairy do-gooder hooey.

The word we've received is that the attitude to human rights, which will now baffle even the carefully tutored eye by being re-defined without ever having been defined, will now be indexed to the more general attitude to the nation in question.

The idea seems to be that human rights will be shifted down below sundries on the priorities list in the case of a friendly nation, whereas in the case of a non-friendly nation, violations will be highlighted and incorporated in popular song. I say this is what the idea seems to be, because at this stage I'm not sure someone hasn't been at the telex machine again.

But just in case it is true, let's look at an example. Let's say that there's a human right being violated somewhere in a place like, say for argument's sake, El Salvador. I know this is ridiculous, but let's just assume that it's happening, simply for the sake of the discussion.

In fact if we're going to be hypothetical, let's assume that El Salvador hasn't got a very good record in the human rights area. Let's just pretend for a moment that it's got a very bad record.

Now, if the government of El Salvador tended to be a friendly one, then obviously there'd be no violation of human rights. So let's assume that the word 'friendly' doesn't really mean 'friendly'. Let's say it means something else. In fact let's say everything means something else. Either that, or let's say nothing. I don't much care.

I'm prepared not to say anything if that's the view of the meeting, and I'm sure that if people's human rights are violated *enough*, they can be relied upon not to breathe a word of it.

B52s

Some people voiced concern that the American air force planes might carry dangerous bombs into Australia. It was essential that the true position be formally outlined.

Gidday. Now look, I might have given you the wrong impression on this business of our defence. I didn't mean to convey the idea that we don't know what's going on. We do. What bothers us is that we don't know enough about what's going on.

I'm not saying it bothers us very much. But it does just linger in the back of the mind, and I won't deny that we're taking steps to find out either a little more about what's going on, or why it is that we don't at this stage know very much about what's going on.

As I say, we're not in a blind flap about this. It's a simple mistake. Somebody's obviously just mislaid the file. We're going through the place now and I'm pretty confident we'll turn something up sooner or later.

One of the problems is that these B52s we've been asked to look out for don't show up on the big board at the southern end of the main concourse, and as a result we don't really have an estimated time of arrival for them. And more specifically, of course, we don't know a lot about the cargo.

Not that this is a big worry really. There's not a lot they could be carrying. I know there's some concern that they might be carrying a few peaceful purposes, but I think it's important to put this concern into some sort of perspective by looking at the subtleties of international strategic deployment.

Obviously the Americans don't want anyone to know what's coming through the Darwin office, in case anything goes wrong and it happens a bit late to make the papers. If they tell us when they're shipping the peaceful purposes in, someone else might drop a pretty bad accident on the place, and that, of course, is the last thing anyone wants to happen.

If, on the other hand, they just fly the planes in with a spare parts manual and the movie for Saturday, they might fool someone into *thinking* they've got a load of peaceful purposes. The difference here is that although we'd still have a pretty bad accident on our hands, the deception will have been a tactical success. Qualified certainly, but nevertheless resounding, I should think.

F111A PURCHASE

The controversy about the F111 has raged for many years. The fact remains that it is a remarkable aircraft.

Gidday. Now I don't know whether or not you've been keeping an eye on the requisition forms that have been floating in from ordnance lately for stamping, but we've ordered an extra third of a dozen assorted second-hand F111A aircraft from GHQ, to replace some of the stuff that's tumbled out of the nimbus during exercises designed to frighten our enemies into thinking we'd got hold of a plane that would fly.

Not only will these planes replace the old ones, but by bringing them into Australia we'll prevent them from crashing in America, and *they* might frighten *their* enemies into thinking they've developed a plane that isn't going to crash without leaving the country.

So the benefits are obvious from a strategic point of view, and from an Australian point of view it's an investment in the American point of view.

I appreciate that the F111 has been under a bit of a cloud in recent years, but this is the E-type model, and we're expecting any problems to iron themselves out fairly early on. Some of our other aircraft have ironed themselves out pretty comprehensively, and only by trial will we be able to locate error.

In the meantime we'll have a fleet of aircraft that are so sophisticated that human understanding can't cope with what's wrong with them. The cost of the four additions is

$60 million, which is extremely reasonable, although that doesn't include the price of the steel helmets you'll be all receiving in the mail.

These are to be worn at all times, inside or out.

It's a psychological thing really. They won't be of any very noticeable medical benefit if you're actually struck by one of these planes. But they will make you feel better about moving about during peacetime.

If by chance one does come down somewhere near you, just go to any post office and fill out an F111 Crash form, I think it's a 41F/9 from memory, but they should be able to tell you. And as soon as we get the form through here, we'll send away for another one.

EL SALVADOR

When the United States Government
decided to enforce its human rights
policy in South America, it was suggested
that El Salvador might become another
Vietnam. It became necessary to point
out exactly why this view was wrong.

Gidday. Now, look. About El Salvador. I know a lot of people are concerned. I realise there are certain traps we should be wary of, and obviously we're determined not to repeat the mistakes we might have made in previous years.

El Salvador is going to be different. We're going to win this one.

That's not meant to sound like sabre-rattling. It simply represents a determination not to be defeated.

In fact we don't think that's the sort of exercise this is anyway. Basically, all we're going to do is protect the present government from violent overthrow. And it doesn't take a lot of military know-how to recognise that one of the more logical responses to this problem is to get in there and underthrow the opposition.

We haven't got a lot of people down there. At this stage there's hardly anyone down there. You could shoot a cannon down the middle of the main street and not hit an American from dawn till sundown.

Obviously we're not at all happy about the way things are going in El Salvador, but at the moment we've confined ourselves to sending in military equipment and two dozen area sales managers who are down there on a bush-walk.

We are planning to spend an extra $26 million on a wide range of assorted hardware, and naturally we'll need to send a few of our people down there to make sure the weapons are used to prevent any further fighting.

As I understand it, the Great Ronaldo has decided not to talk to the Russians about the problems and differences between them because there are too many problems and differences between them.

And I don't know what Bonzo has got in his hand, but I can't see him playing under that.

CHARACTER ANALYSIS

Gidday. Now today's little lecture will concern itself with the analysis of the human character.

I remember some years ago when I was in London, taking the waters and some of the whiskies, I had my palm read by a charming woman who wore a red curtain and spoke with a series of very thick accents.

She told me I'd been on a long journey across many thousands of miles, and that I was in a new place, and had left my old place many thousands of miles behind me, and that I didn't have many of my immediate family with me, and that they were all away across the seas and the clouds and past many rivers, and were in a distant place a great many

157

thousands of miles away, and that one day I would return whence I had come in the first instance, and it would be a journey of major proportions involving the traversing of many lands and kingdoms, to a distant place situated many thousands of miles away, and nowhere at all adjacent to where we were at the time, which happened to be just near the main entrance of the Highgate Cemetery. As you can see this is a fairly penetrating piece of divining and it affected me very deeply to the tune of £1 sterling.

Of course there are many other ways of ascertaining the nature of someone's character, and Handwriting's one of the better ones.

If you write off about a ten yard run-up, and you do huge swirling loops that knock the phone off the desk, and you can fit about three words of your neatest RSVP writing on to a sheet of foolscap, then you'll tend to be a relatively confident person; and you're quite possibly the sort of person who inspires either fear, or laughter. If your writing is very small and extremely faint, and you write only because you're too shy to say anything, then you're probably a shy person and your handwriting will tend to be on the small side.

Now all this might strike you as being perceptive to a quite remarkable degree, but it's all there in the handwriting. I just read it, I'm only saying what I see.

You can also feel people's heads, although you will find that in a lot of cases people will want to feel yours back, and at about that stage it's a good idea to go on a long journey to a distant place many thousands of miles away.

HUMAN MEMORY

Gidday. Now I'd like to outline for you the Fred Dagg Theory of the Human Memory, which has already leaked out in certain circles and has set the scientific world back on its pseudopodia.

The contention is predicated on the nature of human pleasure, which we in the Faculty of Previous Existence believe to be closely linked to the memory in the following fashion.

When we see something that gives us pleasure, say for example a pleasing view from a window, or as we scientists call it, 'A', the experience triggers off in the mind, or the brain, or certainly in the body, or somewhere near the body, or possibly somewhere else, the recalling of a similar view observed at some previous time, and that at that previous time the observer was happy. This means that the memory is not necessarily a memory of the view from the window, or 'A', but a memory of pleasure itself, which is activated by the visual experience of the clapping of the peepers on 'A'.

There seems no difficulty in accepting that this quintessential happiness can originate to some extent prior to egress from the womb, as witness the tendency to assume the foetal position in moments of stress in early childhood or advanced inebriation.

Research is being done even as I speak into the possibility that the pleasure is remembered from a stage prior even to conception. In fact even in scientific circles it is now widely accepted that there very often *is* some pleasure prior to conception.

159

This means that there may be an argument to be made out for claiming that we experience someone else's pleasure, or that someone else experiences ours, or as we call it, The Life of Riley Syndrome. Of course, the implications of this are far-reaching and it's fair to say the whole area of study is still at this stage in someone else's infancy. I'll let you know of any further developments as they come to hand.

I'll let myself out. You just rest, I'll see you later.

BREEDING NOBEL PRIZE-WINNERS

The suggestion that a dynasty of Nobel Prize-winners might be established by medical science, raised certain fundamental questions.

Gidday. Now I suppose you noticed, as I did, a flurry of publicity in recent weeks concerning the business of inseminating suitable dams with millions of little squiggles from the trousorial section of Nobel Prize-winners. And I think there are one or two things that need to be said.

Firstly, if there's going to be some attempt to establish a dynasty of these characters, I think the viva-vas-deferens brigade is going to have to pay some attention to the distaff side, on the two very crucial grounds that women are often mentioned as winners of the Award, and that certain difficulties arise in the isolation of their essence for purely stud purposes. It seems that the idea as it stands at the moment is to perpetuate the line of male winners, and allow women only a very haphazard long shot in the open freestyle.

But the major problem, and I think it over-rides all other considerations, is that rather than continue with the pedigree, we should look very carefully at knocking any further breeding on the head altogether.

It's fairly obvious, even to members of the laity, that the fact that the northern hemisphere's stiff with life-sapping conical whizzbangs all pointing at each other, and bombs, and jars full of bugs, and other things we don't even know about, is due largely to the courageous march of science. And a great number of Laureates have won the peace prize for forging ahead in these only very slightly peaceful areas.

Of course you can't blame everyone since Newton for the H-bomb, but I'll be sorely tempted if one ever lands anywhere near me. And if dear old Nobel, whom I recall quite clearly even today, padding about the lab with his glasses up in his hair, felt badly about developing dynamite, and established a peace prize to make himself feel better about it, then clearly genius is still regarded as being more important than apologising for the effects of it.

I think in all fairness, Australia should be awarded the Nobel Prize for Retailing, for its decision to market uranium for peaceful purposes. Although if this means introducing suitable women to frozen Australian governmental semen, I can see property values taking a bit of a pounding in the known world.

THE TWO-AIRLINE POLICY

Australia's internal air policy provided an excellent example of the ability of market forces to determine the extent to which they are controlled.

Gidday. Now I'd like to have a word or two with you about the two-airline policy which is in effect a long-standing arrangement to ensure that if the consumer misses one plane, he can be secure in the knowledge that if he'd got there five minutes earlier, he'd have missed the other one.

The policy is under a bit of a cloud at the moment because the two airlines involved have decided to compete with one another for business. It's a fairly pagan form of competition, but I think you'd have to say that in some sense it isn't *not* competition. Or at least it isn't entirely *not* competition in every respect.

The airlines are supposed to create the illusion of competition without actually permitting the competitive element to stand in the way of the fact that if one of them wins, it's a mountainous victory for all that's decent, and if the other one wins, they have to go back and start again.

What's happened recently is that everyone's gone out and bought the newest planes on the market, with great fats on the back and a big stripe up the bonnet, and each is accusing the other of having made a major miscalculation which is going to cost the people of Australia a fortune.

That is to say, a bigger fortune than paying for two half-empty planes to leave everywhere on the hour and near the hour, just about every hour, and follow each other to everywhere else, and use different carparks when they get there just to make it look as if free enterprise hasn't been delayed due to maintenance.

Personally, I hope that if there's been a mistake on the order forms, it hasn't happened in the white corner, because if it has, the boys in the blue corner will be brought back to the starting gates and forced to make a mistake of similar magnitude, just to give everyone an equal opportunity to take advantage of open competition.

That's the thing about the two-airline policy. It's got to be revised all the time in case it works.

REAL ESTATE

Gidday. Now the Fred Dagg Careers Advisory Bureau has already done more than enough to secure its place in the social history of this once great nation, but I think this report is probably among its more lasting achievements.

In essence it outlines how to go about the business of being a real estate agent, and as things stand at the moment if you're not a real estate agent, then you're being a fool to yourself and a burden to others.

Like so many other jobs in this wonderful society of ours, the basic function of the real estate agent is to increase the price of the article without actually producing anything, and as a result it has a lot to do with communication, terminology, and calling a spade a delightfully bucolic colonial winner facing north and offering a unique opportunity to the handyman.

If you're going to enter the real estate field you'll need to acquire a certain physical appearance which I won't bore you with here, but if you've got gold teeth and laugh-lines round your pockets, then you're through to the semis without dropping a set.

But the main thing to master, of course, is the vernacular, and basically this works as follows: there are three types of houses; glorious commanding majestic split-level ultra-modern dream homes, which are built on cliff-faces; private bush-clad inglenooks which are built down holes; and very affordable solid family houses in much sought-after streets, which are old gun-emplacements with awnings. A cottage is a caravan with the wheels taken off. A panoramic, breathtaking, spectacular, or magnificent view is an indication that the house has windows, and if the view is unique, there's probably only one window.

I have here the perfect advertisement for a house, so we'll go through it and I'll point out some of the more interesting features, so here we go, mind the step.

'Owner transferred reluctantly instructs us to sell' means the house is for sale. 'Genuine reason for selling' means the house is for sale. 'Rarely can we offer' means the house is for sale. 'Superbly presented delightful charmer' doesn't mean anything really, but it's probably still for sale. 'Most attractive immaculate home of character in prime dress-circle position' means that the thing that's for sale is a house. 'Unusual design with interesting and intriguing solidly built stairs' means the stairs are in the wrong place. 'Huge spacious generous lounge commands this well serviced executive residence' means the rest of the house is a rabbit-warren with rooms like cupboards. 'Magnificent well-proportioned large convenient block with exquisite garden' means there's no view but one of the trees had a flower on it the day we were up there. 'Privacy, taste, charm, space, freedom, quiet, away from it all location in much sought-after cul-de-sac situation' means it's not only built down a hole, it's built at the very far end of the hole. 'A must for you artists, sculptors and potters' means that only a lunatic would consider living in it. '2/3 bedrooms with possible in-law accommodation' means it's got two bedrooms and a tool shed. 'Great buy, ring early for this one, inspection a must, priced to sell, new listing, see this one now, all offers considered, good value, be quick, inspection by appointment, view today, this one can't last, sole agents, today's best buy' means the house is still for sale, and if ever you see 'investment opportunity' turn away very quickly and have a go at the crossword.

ADVERTISING

Gidday. I must say that we down at the Bureau had a very enjoyable time researching this one.

On the first day, we kicked off with a light lunch that lasted about five hours, then we took the idea over to our creative department who recommended we get in touch with some of the people over in concepts. Concepts went out and had a decent-sized lunch on it, and came back with a story-board which we tested in an open-ended, one-to-one sample situation. Actually, we did this in Bangkok – we were going up there anyway for lunch so it wasn't too far out of our way. Next we went to Paris for a couple of days to throw a few ideas around and get some different coloured felt pens, and then on to Rio for lunch.

On the way back I ran into a bloke who used to be AE with O & M before we both went across to Burnetts when Pattersons had burgled the MDA account from Hertz Walpole. He's now creative director with Silvergold Finklestein Gifilterfish and Baumbaum, and works out of New York. So we went over to his office for a short snort before lunch and he went over the whole concept with a fine tooth comb, right down to the media schedules and the market mixes. And ultimately he recommended that I conduct this lecture on the Don Lane Show, the Mike Walsh Show and the Willesee programme coupled with in-store promotion, pop-out full-colour, relief-poster point-of-sale material and a radio and TV saturation campaign featuring John Newcombe doing a Bee Gees number with the critical message in the gaps between the choruses.

It's a nice idea. I like it, I like it a lot, and after lunch I'll decide what to do about it.

CRICKET

The catch of the 1981–82 cricket season was taken at the MCG by Martin Snedden. Running in from deep mid-wicket, Snedden dived several yards and took a magnificent catch to fail to dismiss Greg Chappell.

Gidday. Now I've waited a while before making this statement because I thought somebody else might get in and unveil the observation before this.

It occurs to me, following Greg Chappell's apparent inability to effect a fairly elementary right turn and wander off towards the pavilion before he's been caught at least twice, that maybe I wasn't looking at things the right way.

A proper assessment in the light of recent events shows quite clearly that Greg Chappell has never been out at all at any stage of his career; and that he just decides sometimes that he's a bit tired, or he's got to catch a plane or something, and he consents to vacate the arena if the bowler manages to lift the stumps completely out of the ground and deposit them in a canvas bag behind the sightscreen.

I must say that having seen him play a few games over the years, thinking back, I've certainly never seen him actually dismissed. I've seen him caught, and I've seen him bowled, and unless my memory's drifting to starboard, I've even seen him caught and bowled a couple of times, but I don't think I've ever seen him actually dismissed.

As I say, he's left the ground on occasions, but he probably has his own reasons for these things, and I don't pry. I think it's his own business. They must get thirsty after a while out there, and I know from personal experience that being caught at deep mid-wicket can certainly sap your confidence, especially if you've been hit in the leg a few times out in that area in front of the wickets.

Of course, there are other considerations. Obviously there are times when he simply thinks it wouldn't be a bad idea if someone else had a turn. But you learn to pick these occasions. You can normally see him signalling to Trevor from the non-striker's end.

This is one of the great things about cricket. Despite the money and all the controversy that's come to surround it, it's still a game he feels he can take the family to.

WIMBLEDON PRESS COVERAGE

Until 1981, the Wimbledon Men's Final had for some time been a series of action-replays of itself. The world's sporting press was beginning to crack.

Gidday. Now I'd like to have a few words with you on behalf of the federation of sports journalists. There's some feeling within the organisation that there were times during the Wimbledon championships when the natural enthusiasm of the period took perhaps too strong a hold on the style of reportage.

The meeting voted, for instance, that it regretted some slight overuse of the expression 'ice cold Swedish tennis genius Bjorn Borg, the greatest player in the history of everything anywhere in the universe'.

This resolution was carried by acclamation. Hats were thrown in the air. Restraint went out the window. Many reporters flew their families in and wept openly when the result became more and more inevitable.

It was also suggested that the phrase 'Genius Super-Bjorn the unbeatable Swedish phenomenon' be dropped from official bulletins in the future, because 'ill-mannered Crypto-brat', the 'universally unpopular American upstart Super-jerk', nearly beat him in the 'most brilliant tennis match anyone's ever seen anywhere at any time ever in the history of recorded time at this or any other venue in any final of any championship at any stage since the beginning of our galaxy'.

I might say at this point, I was actually against these decisions myself. I thought they were a bit hysterical. I stand by the reports. I think these things needed to be said.

Something certainly needs to be said, or we'll be left with a fortnight of incompetent umpires being glared at by millionaire schoolchildren, and then Borg falling to his knees, Borg kissing the cup, and 'Super-genius-tennis Swede-Ace-genius in Australia later in year for Grandslam attempt on Super-open'.

I don't think I could take it. Someone might beat him at Flushing Meadows, of course. It's completely impossible. But it might happen.

THE CAR THAT RAN ON WATER

Some of the world's most valuable ideas come from Queensland. In 1980, a man developed a car that ran on water. On the day of the demonstration someone mislaid the key. The idea of a car that runs on water remains a valuable idea.

Gidday. Now I'd like to have a word or two with you today about this new car of mine that runs on air and whistles 'Beautiful Dreamer'; and the reason I mention it at all is that I really do feel we owe you an explanation.

The bloke with the key simply wasn't there. I was simply there of course; some of my engineers were simply there, and the Premier, Mr Gerald Mander, was there as simply as I've seen him in years.

If he hadn't been, we'd probably all have been arrested, as there were more than three of us all outside together on a day of the week, which can get pretty perilous up here, unless you're a re-development scheme, or a how to vote card with thumb prints all over it. But none of this alters the value of the car itself.

I know it's become accepted behaviour in the smart set for all manner of flapper and wide-boy to go for bit of a deride here, and generally try to extract the Mikhail from the whole exercise, but I'll tell you now, these people will be laughing up the other side of the fizzer when we get the thing to Sydney and open the boot.

Because there are two things in the boot; the bloke with the key and the actual central-fueling-mechanism. Obviously you can't see that at the moment, because until it's patented, I'd be a fool to myself if I started showing people how the power is generated.

I can outline for you the broad principle of the thing.

The air is taken into the fuel production unit, where it's given what I can only really describe as the fright of its life by being turned into either conventional high octane petroleum, or LPG.

Now I needs must draw a bit of a veil over precisely how this is done, although any physicists working in the area of ultra-high pressure fuel conversions will probably be familiar with the field we're talking about here. Magic.

AGENT ORANGE

The Australian Government's attitude to
Agent Orange has been an example
to us all.

Gidday. Now I'd like, if I may, to make just one or two
points relating to Agent Orange.

I've dealt with this subject at some length on several
previous occasions, and I don't really want to go right back
over the whole thing. But if I can take up for a moment, the
question of Australian use of the stuff in Vietnam, I repeat
that there is no evidence that I know of that any strategic or
specifically military use was made of Agent Orange by any
Australian personnel.

Neither do I have any record in my hand at the moment that any Australians were involved in the war in Vietnam.

In fact, there is no proof at this time sitting on my desk between the phone and the out-tray, that what went on in Vietnam was a war at all.

And if I were to tell you that right now there is no notification written on the inside of this hole in the ground that there's ever been any sort of warfare, or killing, or cruelty, or barbarism, or insanity, or lack of humanity, anywhere at all in the history of the universe, then I must ask you to believe me.

Of course, the notion that there's some sort of immorality in using things like Agent Orange during war time presupposes that there are certain rules attaching to the conducting of hostilities, and that these laws are internationally agreed to and universally observed. And I'm afraid that if you go along with this idea, you haven't done very well in your special subject.

It is true that we had a certain amount of Agent Orange in use in some areas, but it was only to keep the weeds down on the base.

I think a lot of people forget that these things can be used for peaceful purposes.

Not that I'm suggesting this is a good thing. In fact, there's no evidence with my department at the moment that it's a thing at all. In fact, there's nothing written on the inside of my lower colon to indicate that anything's anything at all.

I'll get out of your way now, hand me the shovel.

DESIGN FOR THE NEW PARLIAMENT

The competition for a design for Australia's new Parliament House drew entries from architects and visionaries all over the world.

Gidday. Now I'd like to have a few words with you about the rather surprising news that we didn't win the competition for the new parliament building. I say we, because I entered the thing with Frank Lloyd Wright-Mate, whom I've known for donkey's years, and for whose expertise in this area I have the very highest respect.

And I don't want this to sound like sour grapes, but I really do think the boomerang idea is not very exciting. Not only is it not a new idea – there are curved buildings all over the world, and of course the shape of the boomerang wasn't entirely lost on the Nash family – it also isn't very Australian.

At least not by comparison with our proposal, and I'll tell a little of what I mean.

I'm not doing this to start a public outcry. I accept absolutely that the judges' decision is final, and I'm not going to go around walking into any correspondents, but I do think we perhaps all ought to be aware of what might have been.

Imagine if you will, a building in the form of a didgeridoo, set in a field of witchety-grubs, which would have been the car parks, and a big fat one under a log for a canteen. A 2000 foot kangaroo holding the staff lunch rooms and the broom cupboard. On top of the kangaroo we've got the central complex. The main building is Shane Gould. She's 3000 feet long, and supported by Dawn Fraser at one end, housing the opposition facilities, and Walter Lindrum at the other, holding Shane's head, which as you may know, is an observation deck. On Shane's back is Heather McKay housing the lifts up to Don Bradman standing on her shoulders with the House of Reps in his bat-handle and the Senate up the back of his shirt.

A lot of people think this is a bit garish, a bit busy, and perhaps a bit loud. But there is another one, and at 17 miles high this is the tallest building in the world.

It's the Fairfax family holding Rupert Murdoch aloft, and Rupert's holding Packer up on his shoulders, and Packer's got a big rope and he's pulling some of the Fairfaxes up on to his head.

So, in one go, we'd have a monument to all that's good and decent, plus a perpetual motion machine, plus we'll have got rid of the need to have a parliament at all.

INSURANCE

Gidday. It's about time I shared with you a collection of divers pearls about how to run an insurance company, and as this country is a shrine to insurance, it's probably a good idea to know how they work even if you don't actually want to run one.

The insurance company functions on two of the system's most hallowed precepts – greed, and fear of lack of greed. The insurance company capitalises on the natural greed of the gullible, or the insured, as he's sometimes called, and then it worries him that he isn't being quite greedy enough.

If everything that's insured was stolen or burnt down, there wouldn't be enough money ever printed in the history of the world to pay for it. But this doesn't matter because insurance companies are really selling something called 'peace of mind', which is not related to the real world except when you're paying for it. 'Peace of mind' is actually a relatively marvellous thing to sell because you've still got it after you've sold it.

Now let's take the case of what's sometimes risibly referred to as life insurance. The insurance company agrees to pay interest on your money at the very advantageous rate of minus 2000 per cent over a period of, say, 30 years. Now this means that every year, or half year, or month or whenever the computer tells you to, you pay the company an amount of money. The insurance company uses this money to invest in business enterprises like buildings and trafficking in young virgins so that it can pay you back. Should you want the money before you die or before the feeling goes in your happy valve, then they calculate something called the 'surrender value'. This is worked out by adding up all the money you've put in and hiding it under the floorboards before you arrive. When you get there, they demonstrate that as long as you're paying in, you've got a tax savings of a million dollars a week. You then surrender, and the insurance company gives to you the bus fare home and an evening paper. So as you can see, the way the deck is stacked at the moment, the faster you turn yourself into a registered insurance company, the better.

TENNIS

Gidday. Now today I want to waylay you with another suggestion about how to show the weekend who's boss, and this method fulfils most of the requirements of a leisure activity as laid down in the Geneva Convention.

It's time consuming to a point where you can actually think you're busy, it's tiring, it involves special clothing and equipment and in general terms it's a 100 per cent bona fide waste of time, and I refer, of course, to the ancient and revered art of tennis.

First of all, you'll need a tennis court, and if you play your cards right, you can spend till about Sunday lunchtime waiting for one to be vacated by three or four big brunhildes who've been whacking around on it since April, rallying for service.

180

By the time you get a court it'll be raining, and there'll be a Force 9 blowing leaves and silt in from Asia. This will carry the ball over the net, the wire fence and a seven-acre subdivision at the back, the net will have wound itself into a thin line of black string, so you can't tell whether your shots are going under it or over it, and you only find out where it is when you hurl yourself forward to smash a lob, and it bends you in the trousers and drops you on your back between the tramlines.

You should really wear whites and have a good racquet, but if you couldn't raise a mortgage in time, you can generally get away with an honest attempt.

A pair of white shorts you once washed with some red curtains, and now have a blotchy pink aspect to them, and a painting rag with armholes is often quite acceptable, if you've got shoes the same colour and a good hat.

A good hat is crucial, and if you can't get one of those visor arrangements from an old New York newspaper editor, you might get by with a sweatband, which is like a sock you wear round your bonce to keep your brains from sliding out your ears.

Always remember that the best sports gear has two stripes down it, so whatever you've got, get a good thick biro and plant a couple of stripes on it so you look like a pre-war postman, and you'll be OK in the sartorial department.

The next thing is the game, and although it's the least important aspect of the whole exercise, it's as well to know a couple of the basic rules, in case the Rosewalls on the next court ask you whether their last serve was a let or an inwards 1½ with a degree of difficulty of 2·4.

The way to score is relatively simple, and once you've played a few games, you'll pick it up, no trouble.

The first person serves, and that's called a double-fault, and so on until you get to the point where all the balls are in the blackberries up behind the carpark. Then the person to the left of the dealer says juice, and you all go and do that, and it's fun from there on.

WRITING AN AUTOBIOGRAPHY

Gidday. Now I'd like to have a few words with you today about writing an autobiography.

This is a highly recommended form of leisure activity, as it takes up large chunks of time and if you're a slow writer or you think particularly highly of yourself, you can probably whistle away a year or two. A cursory glance at most autobiographies available on the open market will convince you that they were written to fill in a bit of time.

If you feel that your life hasn't really been as fascinating as it might have been, don't let it worry you. If you reckon you've had a dull patch, say you didn't do much of any great moment between 1900 and about last Wednesday, don't be downhearted. All you've got to do is make it up. Pad it out a bit.

You'll get away with it if you remember the cardinal rules of autobiography.

Always take issue with Ruskin on a couple of minor points. Any points will do. And if you don't know what Ruskin said, don't worry, neither does anyone else. It's not important to know what he said. Just remember to take issue with him.

Always mention your travels. Say how impressed you were on first seeing the Alps, or the Moors, or a few cathedrals, or a famous gallery somewhere. Or if you want to be an iconoclast, say how unimpressed you were. But somehow you've got to work in your impressions one way or another. If you've never actually seen the Alps, there are photos of them everywhere. Have a look and see what you think.

Always spend a fair bit of time mulling over the title. Titles are very important, and you can't be too careful. Puns are very good titles, of course, and very bad puns are extremely good. Make a list of excruciating puns, and the ones you reject will do you very nicely as chapter headings. Another favourite is a piece of Shakespeare or some other literature of great profundity. Always use half a line, never a complete quotation. Something like 'Prithee nuncle whist lo my leige waits without' is no good at all, but 'Prithee nuncle whist, Prithee nuncle whist lo, whist lo my leige, lo my leige waits, my leige waits without' or just plain 'Prithee nuncle', are all crackers.

The only thing you need now is photographs. Photographs give a life substance and are a handy device for separating the front part of the book from the back part. You'll need a few photos of your family, and you should leave these in the oven overnight in a mixture of cold tea and aircraft glue so they have about them the requisite appearance of the tranquil days of yore.

You'll need one photo of yourself with someone famous, and by famous I mean more famous than you. You'll need a couple of shots of buildings, one of a picnic and, of course, one of the Alps.

So as you can see, it's not a difficult business and remember this is also your big opportunity to explain what a wonderful person you are, and how you've been consistently misunderstood by your friends and mentors, and most of all by riff-raff like Ruskin and the Alps.

YACHTING

Gidday. Now I'd like to wave my dulcets about today on a subject of major fascination for all leisure-minded people, and I'm referring here, of course, to yachting. Yachting is a well-established method of putting a weekend under your belt, and it has the added advantage of causing total lack of recall. Whole slabs of your life can become complete blanks.

There are several basic requirements in this area, and it's as well to be familiar with the conventions and the terminology if you are going to spend any amount of time before the mast.

Firstly, you'll need a white polo-neck jumper, and a short yellow nylon raincoat, preferably one with a few badges sewn up the arm. This should get you into any yacht club, and if your income's over about $15 000 a week, you should be able to hold your own in conversation until you pick up the vernacular and feel completely at home.

You'll have to know the difference between starboard and port of course. Port is a rather furry beverage and I think starboard is made from gin and crème de menthe. The starboard side is where the gin's kept and Port Said is a place in North Africa. If anyone mentions Port Said, you're a fair bit out of your way, and you probably won't be in the office until well after smoko on the Monday.

The mast is a tall arrangement in the middle for steadying yourself against, and the sails are a series of big sheets that indicate the wind direction, so you can lean into the updraft and prevent yourself from being washed away.

If the wind changes dramatically, someone will tell you to go about, which simply means turning yourself around and toasting the land out the other side.

185

Lee O means everyone has to down whatever they're drinking, and have whatever the captain's having.

The bow is a mixture of rum and cloves and Malvern water, and a stern is a little bit like a black Russian with a dash of retsina. To splice something is to add lemon. An upper fore mizzen tops'l halyard is a gin sling with a small piece of rope in it, and cleat is a nip of gin taken straight out of bottle cap, with nothing added.

That's really about all you'll need to know at this stage; not many novices can last much longer than a few starboards, a couple of sterns and a cleat or two and if you splice the upper fore mizzen tops'l halyard, it'll all be over in the first round.

Anyway, give it a go and if you don't take to yachting the first time you try it, there are plenty of places you can go to dry out.

SKI-ING

Gidday. I'd like to have a word or two with you today about an activity which is enjoying its customary seasonal popularity even as I speak, and I refer here, of course, to ski-ing, which is a very old pastime and, I think, deservedly so.

Ski-ing was discovered by a Swiss gentleman during the middle-ages, I think he was about 45. He lived up the Matterhorn, and he fell over one night while putting the cat out. He also discovered the ski-jump, the somersault, the avalanche and the greenstick fracture in the clavicle.

Nowadays of course, ski-ing has become available to pretty well anyone in society with a thirst for adventure and about $100000. Mind you, since its advent as a purely sportive activity, it has garnered unto its person several new characteristics.

One important innovation that has been made is the discovery that being up a mountain can cause a severe dryness in the mouth. This can be alleviated only by drinking, which can cause a severe dryness in the mouth and so it goes on.

Consequently the skis became larger and longer to give the celebrants a better chance of remaining in the vertical, although later on they were given a pair of sticks to help steady them in cases of wind, and believe you me hot wine can be very problematical in that respect.

In severe cases a large full length white leg casing is placed on the ski-er and with that, plus the skis, plus the sticks, it's practically impossible to fall over, even if you're preserved in alcohol.

Now of course there are some people who do actually glide about on the snow, but this is a very dangerous business and should be avoided. I take it we're all familiar with the concept of a mountain, which is a tall arrangement made of rock. Because of the cold at the top of these things, snow and ice are frequently spotted amassing on the outer surface.

What some of these people do is slide down the slippery outer covering of the mountain until they get to the bottom. This, of course, is insane, and therefore extremely popular, particularly with people who've done well in aircraft components and cost accounting.

LATERAL BANKING

Advancements in thought can often be
of great and lasting value to society
as a whole.

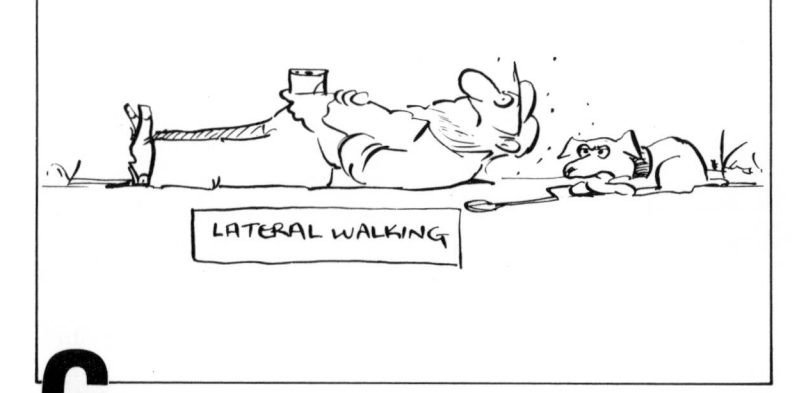

LATERAL WALKING

Gidday. Now I'd like to have a word or two with you about what I think is now widely recognised as the single most important philosophical document of the modern age. And I'm talking here, of course, of the book *Lateral Banking*, which I published some years ago now, under the nom de pseud Edward de Daggo.

As you may subsequently have observed, I've found an industrial application for my work in more recent times, and I'd like to explain roughly how this works, or as I prefer to say 'I'd like to explain its "workness"'.

Obviously one of the most serious problems confronting the industrial nations at the moment is industrial relations, and it's not really possible to put everyone involved in industry through some sort of Relational Interface Therapy, so quite clearly a totally new overall approach is required.

The problems involved in industrial relations differ, of course, with time and place, and one of the difficulties has always been that the solutions have been equally diverse, and the solution in one case might be inapplicable in another. Although it might not be immediately apparent, there is a consistent quality in all the solutions, and that quality can be defined by the fact that to a given degree, those problems have been solved. They have acquired what I call 'solvedness'. And it can be said that rather than having many solutions, we have 'solvedness' which is simply applied in many different ways.

Equally of course, we have 'problemness' which manifests itself in various forms and places.

And in order to counter the now consistent and identifiable 'problemness' with the easily recognisable 'solvedness', and I don't want to go into a needless amount of detail here, it'll only confuse you and this has probably cost you small fortuneness already, but in a nutshell we need to provide a balance between problemness and solvedness, and unfortunately I don't really think at the moment I've got time to run through the concept of balanceness.

Someone will now pass amongst you with millinery, and I'll get back to you about this as soon as you come up with a deposit.